Stylish Quilter

Stylish Quilter

Landauer Publishing, www.landauerpub.com, is an imprint of Fox Chapel Publishing Company, Inc.

Project Team
Acquisitions Editor: Amelia Johanson
Managing Editor: Gretchen Bacon
Editor: Amy Deputato
Copy Editor: Sherry Vitolo
Designer: Wendy Reynolds
Indexer: Jean Bissell

ISBN 978-1-63981-101-4
Library of Congress Control Number: 2024942550

To learn more about the other great books from Fox Chapel Publishing, or to find a retailer near you, call toll-free 800-457-9112, send mail to 903 Square Street, Mount Joy, PA 17552, or visit us at www.FoxChapelPublishing.com.

We are always looking for talented authors. To submit an idea, please send a brief inquiry to acquisitions@foxchapelpublishing.com.

Printed in China
First printing

Stylish Quilter
Traditional Craft for a Modern World

Kiley Ferons · Megan Saenz · Elyse Thompson

Landauer Publishing

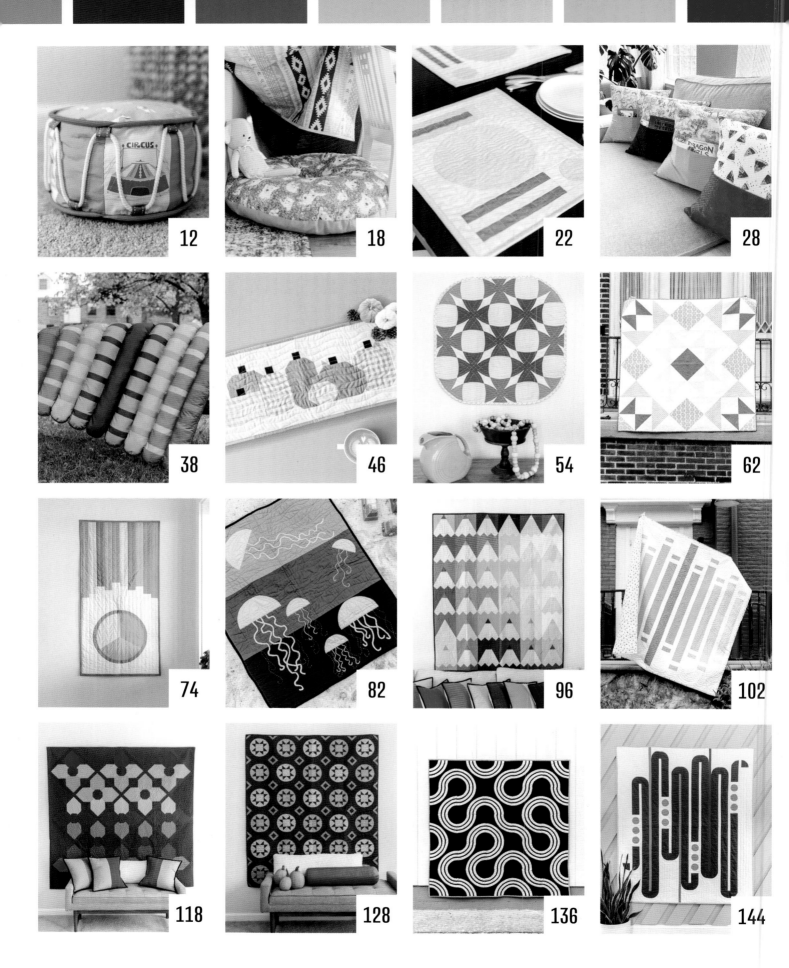

32

68

108

152

Contents

Introduction

As modern design sense continues to influence the direction of quilting in the twenty-first century, a new generation of quilters regularly incorporates their makes into their day-to-day lives. Works of art are displayed on walls; children's rooms are peppered with quilted toys; functional and decorative creations enhance rooms throughout the home with a purposeful sense of style. In *Stylish Quilter,* we've brought a carefully selected collection of patterns together with quilting advice and tutorials designed to infuse your life with the unique sense of style that is a modern quilter's home. Everything is on trend and highlights the techniques every quilter will want to have as part of their skill set if they don't already.

We've organized the patterns by purpose—smaller home projects, decorative pieces, and statement quilts—followed by information on adding tabs, binding, quilt care, and display. This bright, clean, and fresh collection comes to you from us and from a talented group of contributors who, like us, blend their lives with a quilting passion. These pages feature a compilation of the modern and stylish quilting content we brought to our audiences over three years of publishing *Modish Quilter* (an online quarterly that saw its final issue in the spring of 2024). We hope you enjoy this book as we take a look at some of our best work and walk you through the lifestyle of a modern quilter.

—Kiley, Megan, and Elyse

ABBREVIATIONS TO KNOW

F8	fat eighth
FQ	fat quarter
HST	half-square triangle
RST	right sides together
SA	seam allowance
WOF	width of fabric
(...)	numbers in parentheses other than metric measurements usually indicate quantity

The Floor Pouf on page 18 is the perfect piece for creating a cozy corner in your home.

I. Getting into Mental Shape: Five Keys to Help You Prepare for Your Next Quilt Project

Most of the time, starting a new quilting project is exciting. You'll often find yourself wanting to dive right into your fabric stash and start dreaming of what you are going to do with it. But doing so before you are mentally in shape to begin a new project can lead to stress and disaster down the road. This is a common cause of establishing a growing pile of unfinished projects. Follow this guide to mentally prepare for your next project.

Tidy Up

A clean work area creates a clean mind. The leftover fabric trimmings on your cutting mat and scattered rulers in your sewing space are creating clutter both in your work area and in your mind. It's hard to focus on your next project when you're trying to work around the remains of your last project. So, before you even start to consider your next quilt, reset your sewing space. You will feel less stressed afterward, and your mind will be able to think clearly about your next creative idea.

Organize

Organization is key! We know we just told you to go clean your sewing area, but cleaning and organizing are two different skills. Back in 1948, Toyota created the 6S methodology. While it originated in manufacturing, this methodology is now used to manage many types of processes more efficiently. When applied to your sewing room, 6S can deliver you the same results of decreased costs, reduced waste, improved workspace management, and increased productivity. The acronym 6S stands for sort, set, shine, standardize, sustain, and safety. In your sewing space, this would look like organizing your work area and fabric storage to give every fat quarter, ruler, and spool of thread its own dedicated space. Always returning your tools to their proper places means you will always know where they are and what you have. This will give you peace of mind and increase your productivity. What more could you ask for when starting a new project?

Plan Ahead

Go into your new project with a plan. Taking the time to color in a pattern coloring sheet or mocking up a design on your computer will give you focus. Planning out your fabrics will make you more familiar with the project. Reading over the instructions before you begin will give you the confidence to get started.

Manage Your Time

Do what you love in the amount of time you have. There's nothing more difficult than working on a sewing project that doesn't bring joy. If, while you're coloring in your coloring sheet or pulling your fabrics, you fall out of love with what you're working on, it's fine to go back to the drawing board. If you don't look forward to the project, you're not going to want to work on it. Be honest with yourself about what will make you happy, and don't just create to make others happy. You also have to be honest with yourself about how long a project will take. Trying to squeeze two weeks' worth of work into a long weekend is only going to lead to burnout. Plan ahead and give yourself some extra time as a buffer. It's always nice to feel like you've finished a project ahead of schedule!

Do as the French Do

As the French say, *"mise en place,"* which means to have everything cut, laid out, and ready before you begin. After you've become familiar with your pattern, take the time to cut out and label all your pieces before you start sewing. Laying everything out before you begin allows you to confirm that you have everything you need and that each tool or material will be ready to go when you need it.

✳ ✳ ✳ ✳ ✳

Now you're armed with the tools for mental success before you start cutting into your next quilt project. Taking a little time to get ready now will save you hours of fabric-choosing, seam-ripping, and scissor-searching later. You've got this!

The most important part of any new project is the planning stage.

II. Small Projects for Your Home

Usually when people think of quilting, they think of bed quilts. But there are so many other ways to use this art form—and one is to create smaller functional projects for your home. One of the great benefits of smaller quilt projects is that they don't take as much time to complete and can be accomplished in a weekend or even one day. Sometimes you just need a quick and easy project to break up the large quilt projects. This section is full of fun, functional, and/or easy projects that you can use your quilting skills and knowledge to complete quickly. Dive in for fun projects that are sure to impress!

The Scalloped Puff Quilt on page 38 is a smaller project that makes a big statement.

Drum Pillow

By Pascaline of Pompom du Monde

How many of you have made baby quilts for friends or family or maybe even yourselves? This is the perfect project to use up your scraps by creating a matching drum pillow toy for the special child in your life! It's fun and functional, and, best of all, it doesn't require batteries!

Before You Start

- This project can also be made with fabric scraps if you have coordinating colors.

- The seam allowance is ⅜" (1cm) unless otherwise stated.

- The pattern is optimal for all kinds of fabrics.

MATERIALS NEEDED

- Five fat quarters of fabrics in coordinating prints and colors

- 1⅝ yds. (1.5m) of thick piping (I used ⅓" [8mm] piping)

- 2³⁄₁₆ yds. (2m) of thick cording

- Stuffing or fabric scraps

- 7¾" (20cm) medium fusible interfacing

- Fabric scissors

- Fabric marking pen

- Needle

- Thread

- Clips

CUTTING INSTRUCTIONS

- Two drum disks from template

- Eight side panels from template

- Two 2" x 16" (5 x 40cm) fabric strips

1. Apply interfacing to the wrong side of all your pieces except the long strip. This is important to give your pillow more sturdiness.

2. Decide the layout you want for your side panels, then lay them next to each other to keep them in the right order. I've chosen to mix prints and plain fabrics. Take the first and second panel and sew along one long edge with right sides together (RST) and a ⅜" (1cm) seam allowance.

3. Repeat with the next panel until you end up with a long strip. Press the seams open.

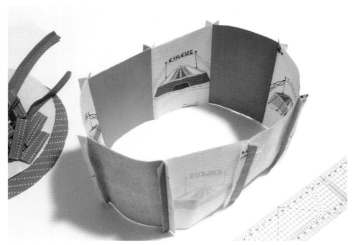

4. Place the last long edges of the first panel and last panel together with RST. Stitch along, leaving a 2¾" (7cm) gap in the middle. This is needed to turn your pillow right side out.

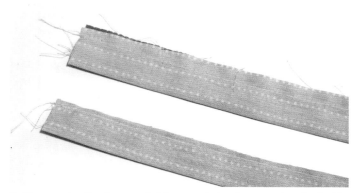

5. To create the loops, fold one of the long strips in half lengthwise, right side in. Sew along the long edge with ⅜" (1cm) seam allowance.

6. Trim your seam allowance to ³⁄₁₆" (4.8mm). To turn your strip right side out, attach a safety pin to one end and slowly channel it into the fabric tube. Gently pull on the other end of the fabric. Once the tube is right

side out, press it flat and divide it into eight pieces, each 2" (5cm) long. Repeat with the other long strip to give you a total of sixteen 2" (5cm) pieces.

7. Take eight of the strips, fold each in half, then place the rough edges along the top rough edge of the side panels, aligning the strips to the seams between each panel. Stitch in place within the seam allowance. Fold the remaining eight pieces in the same way, but place them in the center of the panels, along the bottom rough edge. Stitch in place within the seam allowance.

8. To apply the piping to the side panels, pull and trim ⅜" (1cm) of the cord out from one end. This reduces the bulk where the ends meet. Pin the end of the piping within the seam allowance, then gently turn to align the raw edge to the raw edge of the panel. Pin around the side panels until you get back to the start.

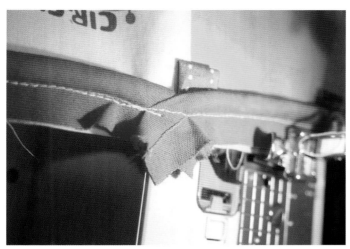

9. Cut your piping to size, then remove ⅜" (1cm) from the other end of the piping. Sew around with a piping foot using a ⅜" (1cm) seam allowance.

10. Repeat with the bottom part of the side panels.

11. On the disk pieces, mark the quarters, then mark again in the center of each quarter to get eight sections. With your side panels facing in, place the disk on top with the right side facing down. Pin in place, matching

your markings with the seams between each panel. To make fitting easier and help your fabric layers lay flat, you can clip the side panels within the seam allowance.

12. Sew slowly to keep the layers aligned until you have closed the top. Repeat this step with the second disk at the bottom. Now you have an inside-out pillow.

13. Using the gap you left in one side panel, turn your pillow to the outside. Stuff it with pillow stuffing or fabric scraps until your pillow feels full, but the top and bottom still feel flat.

14. Using a ladder stitch, close the opening in the side panel.

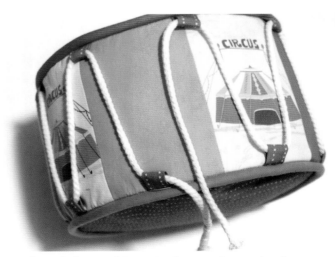

15. Thread the cord into the loops, alternating between the top and bottom to create a zigzag effect.

16. Trim the excess cord and glue both ends together. For a cleaner finish, wrap a small piece of cotton tape around the connection. Glue in place. You're done!

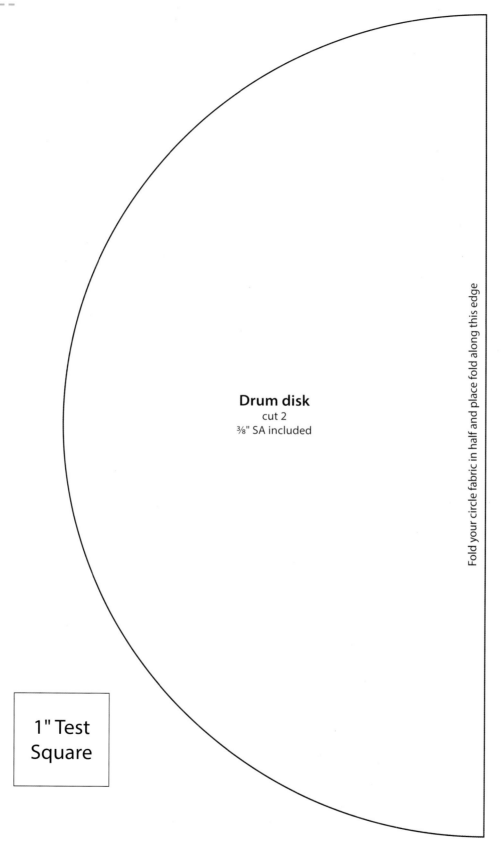

Drum disk
cut 2
⅜" SA included

Fold your circle fabric in half and place fold along this edge

1" Test
Square

1" Test Square

Side panel
cut 8
⅜" SA included

Floor Pouf

By Kiley Ferons of Kiley's Quilting Room

If you have family members like mine, you know that some people can't sit still through a movie! Or maybe you need extra seating at a gathering and don't mind using floor space. This Floor Pouf is the perfect solution to floor seating and lounging. Its large round size makes it perfect for movie nights or get-togethers. And don't forget about furry friends. This is a great option for a homemade dog bed! Whatever you want to use it for—this project is a quick and easy solution for you!

MATERIALS NEEDED

- Two 1 yd. (90cm) cuts of coordinating fabrics
- String, at least 25" (63.5cm) long
- Fabric scissors
- Fabric marking pen (we used Frixion pens)
- Needle
- Thread
- Pins
- Polyfill

This Floor Pouf project is perfect for showcasing your favorite fabric designs.

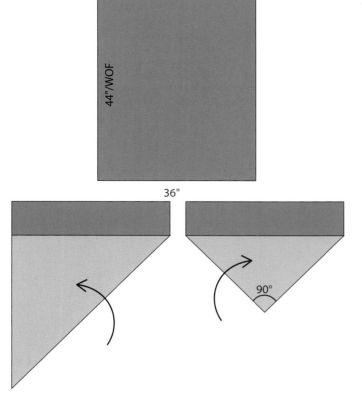

angle to the pen. Tie a knot in the string at the corner. Keeping your finger firmly on this knot, move the pen in an arc over the fabric to mark it. Be sure to hold the string tight and keep the pen straight up and down. Then use fabric scissors to cut the curve through all four layers. Unfold the cut fabric, and you should have a nearly perfect circle! Repeat with the other piece of fabric so that you end up with two fabric circles.

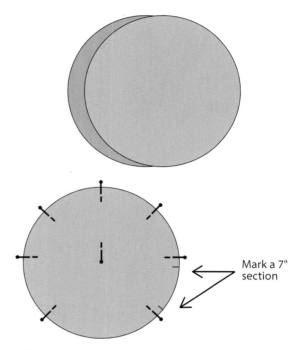

Mark a 7" section

1. Iron your fabrics so you have a nice, smooth surface. Lay out one piece of fabric right side up and fold one corner along the selvage up to the opposite side until the edges—not the corners!—line up. Then take the other corner of the selvage and fold up to the opposite side. The top folded edges should all line up, and the point of the folded triangle should be a 90-degree angle. Repeat with the other piece of fabric.

3. Lay the two circles down with RST. Make sure that the edges all match up. If you need to trim an edge, be sure to match it to the other circle. Pin the edges around the circles. Using the fabric pen, mark off a 7" (17.8cm) section of the edge to leave open for stuffing. Starting at one of the marks, sew a ½" (1.5cm) seam around the circles until you get to the other mark for the opening.

4. Flip your pouf right side out through the 7" (17.8cm) opening and begin stuffing. Be sure not to overstuff it, as it will make it harder to close the opening.

5. To close the opening, first press the edges back ½" (1.5cm) to match the seam line. Using a needle and thread, make tiny hand stitches to close the opening, burying your threads at the start and at the end.

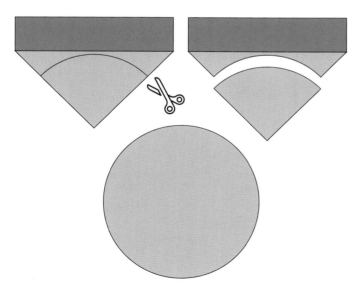

2. Tie the string around your fabric marking pen. Hold the pen about ¼" (6mm) below the top edge of the folded triangle. Pull the string tight at a 90-degree

PROTIP

You can get fancy by
adding a cute button to
the center, cording around
the edges, or even a handle
so you can easily carry
your pouf!

Place-Setting Placemat

By Kiley Ferons of Kiley's Quilting Room

This pattern is not just great for your home decor, it's also a good way to teach kids how to set the table. We feel strongly that dinnertime should be family time. Involving your kids in dinnertime prep gives them a sense of responsibility, accomplishment, and usefulness (despite all the complaining!). These cute placemats are a fun way to get kids excited about helping!

MATERIALS NEEDED

- See Fabric Requirements below
- Rotary cutter
- Cutting mat
- Fabric scissors
- Fabric marking pen
- Needle
- Thread
- Pins
- Quilting ruler
- Batting

Copy and color in the black-and-white diagram to test different color arrangements before you cut!

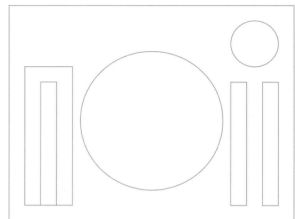

Before You Start

- Make sure to read through all the instructions first.
- Print the templates on pages 26–27 at 100 percent (not "fit to page"). Measure the 1" (2.5cm) reference square on your printout to ensure that everything is the correct size.
- The seam allowance is ¼" (6mm) unless otherwise stated.
- Share your quilt on Instagram with #ModishPlacemat.

FABRIC REQUIREMENTS

	Set of 2	Set of 4	Set of 6	Set of 8
Color 1	⅓ yd. (30.5cm)	⅔ yd. (61cm)	1 yd. (90cm)	1 yd. (90cm)
Color 2	1 F8	1 FQ	1 FQ	1 FQ
Background	½ yd. (45.7cm)	1 yd. (90cm)	1⅓ yds. (1.2m)	2 yds. (1.8m)
Backing	½ yd. (45.7cm)	1 yd. (90cm)	1½ yds. (1.4m)	2 yds. (1.8m)
Binding	⅓ yd. (30.5cm)	⅔ yd. (61cm)	1 yd. (90cm)	1¼ yds. (1.1m)

CUTTING INSTRUCTIONS

	Set of 2	Set of 4	Set of 6	Set of 8
Color 1	Cut one 9½" (24.1cm) x WOF, Subcut: Two 9½" x 9½" (24.1 x 24.1cm) Two 3½" x 3½" (8.9 x 8.9cm) Four 1½" x 8½" (4 x 21.6cm) Two 1½" x 3½" (4 x 8.9cm)	Cut two 9½" (24.1cm) x WOF, Subcut: Four 9½" x 9½" (24.1 x 24.1cm) Four 3½" x 3½" (8.9 x 8.9cm) Eight 1½" x 8½" (4 x 21.6cm) Four 1½" x 3½" (4 x 8.9cm)	Cut three 9½" (24.1cm) x WOF, Subcut: Six 9½" x 9½" (24.1 x 24.1cm) Six 3½" x 3½" (8.9 x 8.9cm) Twelve 1½" x 8½" (4 x 21.6cm) Six 1½" x 3½" (4 x 8.9cm)	Cut three 9½" (24.1cm) x WOF, Subcut: Eight 9½" x 9½" (24.1 x 24.1cm) Eight 3½" x 3½" (8.9 x 8.9cm) Sixteen 1½" x 8½" (4 x 21.6cm) Eight 1½" x 3½" (4 x 8.9cm)
Color 2	Six 1½" x 8½" (4 x 21.6cm)	Twelve 1½" x 8½" (4 x 21.6cm)	Eighteen 1½" x 8½" (4 x 21.6cm)	Twenty-four 1½" x 8½" (4 x 21.6cm)

continued

Background	Cut one 13" (33cm) x WOF, Subcut: Two 13" x 11" (33 x 27.9cm) Four 1½" x 14½" (4 x 36.8cm) Four 1½" x 16½" (4 x 41.9cm)	Cut two 13" (33cm) x WOF, Subcut: Four 13" x 11" (33 x 27.9cm) Eight 1½" x 14½" (4 x 36.8cm) Eight 1½" x 16½" (4 x 41.9cm) Four 1½" x 8½" (4 x 21.6cm)	Cut two 13" (33cm) x WOF, Subcut: Six 13" x 11" (33 x 27.9cm) Six 1½" x 8½" (4 x 21.6cm) Four 3½" x 3½" (8.9 x 8.9cm)	Cut three 13" (33cm) x WOF, Subcut: Eight 13" x 11" (33 x 27.9cm) Eight 4" x 5" (10 x 12.7cm)
	Cut 4" (10cm) x WOF, Subcut: Two 4" x 5" (10 x 12.7cm) Two 3½" x 3½" (8.9 x 8.9cm) Two 1½" x 8½" (4 x 21.6cm)	Cut 4" (10cm) x WOF, Subcut: Four 4" x 5" (10 x 12.7cm) Four 3½" x 3½" (8.9 x 8.9cm)	Cut 16½" (41.9cm) x WOF, Subcut: Twelve 1½" x 16½" (4 x X 41.9cm) Twelve 1½" x 14½" (4 x 36.8cm)	Cut 16½" (41.9cm) x WOF, Subcut: Sixteen 1½" x 16½" (4 x 41.9cm) Twelve 1½" x 14½" (4 x 36.8cm)
			Cut 4" (10cm) x WOF, Subcut: Six 4" x 5" (10 x 12.7cm) Two 3½" x 3½" (8.9 x 8.9cm)	Cut 14½" (36.8cm) x WOF, Subcut: Four 1½" x 14½" (4 x 36.8cm) Eight 3½" x 3½" (8.9 x 8.9cm) Eight 1½" x 8½" (4 x 21.6cm)

Cutting Templates

- Fold all 9½" x 9½" (24.1 x 24.1cm) Color 1 pieces in half. Center the inner plate template and align the straight edge with the fold. Cut along the curve. Keep the circle. This is your inner plate piece.

- Measure 6" (15.2cm) from the bottom on all 11" x 13" (28 x 33cm) background pieces and fold up to crease at that 6" (15.2cm) line. Align the straight edge with the fold and center the background plate template. Cut along the curve. Keep the frame piece. This is your background plate piece.

- Fold all 3½" x 3½" (8.9 x 8.9cm) Color 1 pieces in half. Center the inner cup template and align the straight edge with the fold. Cut along the curve. Keep the circle. This is your inner cup piece.

- Measure 3" (7.6cm) from the bottom on all 4" x 5" (10 x 12.7cm) background pieces and fold up to crease at that 3" (7.6cm) line. Align the straight edge with the fold and center the background plate template. Cut along the curve. Keep the frame piece. This is your background cup piece.

Inset Circles

Following Steps 1–3, put the inner plate piece together with the background plate piece. Then repeat Steps 1 and 2, then follow Step 4, to put the inner cup piece together with the background cup piece.

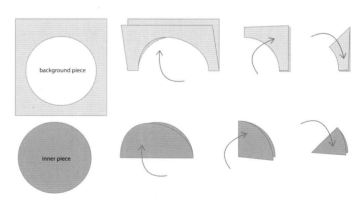

1. Make eight crease marks around the background and Color 1 circles. To do this, fold each piece into eighths and press with your fingers. Be sure to fold the background piece with the right side up and the Color 1 piece with the wrong side up so that the creases will nest when you lay the two pieces together.

2. Lay your pieces down—first the Color 1 piece and then the background piece—both with right sides up. Pull the edge of the background piece into the center so that the creases and raw edges of both pieces are aligned, then pin. Do this with each crease mark all the way around the circles. Sew them together slowly and carefully to avoid puckers. Press the seams.

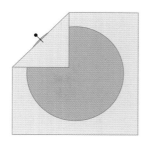

3. Trim the plate piece to 10" x 12" (25.4 x 30.5cm) by measuring 1½" (4cm) from the bottom of the circle and trim the excess. Measure ½" (1.5cm) from both sides of the circle and trim the excess. Measure 2½" (6cm) from the top of the circle and trim the excess, as shown in the illustration.

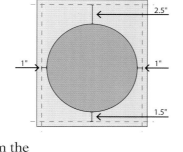

4. Trim the cup piece to 3½" x 4½" (8.9 x 11.4cm) by measuring ½" (1.5cm) away from the top and both sides of the circle. Trim the excess. Measure 1½" (4cm) from the bottom of the circle and trim the excess, as shown in the illustration.

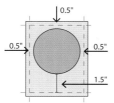

Assembling the Placemat

The following steps are for one placemat. You can chain-piece or repeat steps to complete the number of placemats that you are making.

1. Take two of the 1½" x 8½" (4 x 21.6cm) Color 1 pieces and, with RST, sew one on either side of a 1½" x 8½" (4 x 21.6cm) Color 2 piece. Press the seams to one side. Add a 1½" x 3½" (4 x 8.9cm) Color 1 piece and a 3½" x 3½" (8.9 x 8.9cm) background piece to the top of the strip set.

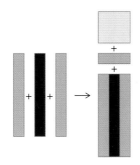

2. Take two 1½" x 8½" (4 x 21.6cm) Color 2 pieces and, with RST, sew one on either side of a 1½" x 8½" (4 x 21.6cm) background piece. Press the seams to one side. Add the cup piece to the top of the strip set.

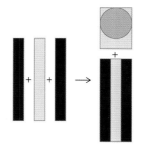

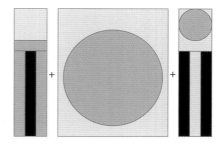

3. Sew the set from Step 1 to the left side of the plate piece and sew the set from Step 2 to the right side of the plate piece, as shown in the illustration. Press the seams in one direction.

4. Sew a 1½" x 16½" (4 x 41.9cm) background piece to the top and bottom of your placemat. Press the seams in. Then sew a 1½" x 14½" (4 x 36.8cm) background piece to the right and left sides of your placemat. Press the seams in.

5. Quilt and bind your placemats as desired. Enjoy!

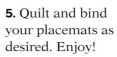

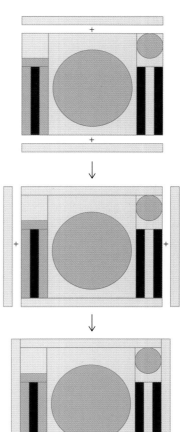

Templates

Print templates at 100% scaling. Use the reference square as a guide.

1" Test
Square

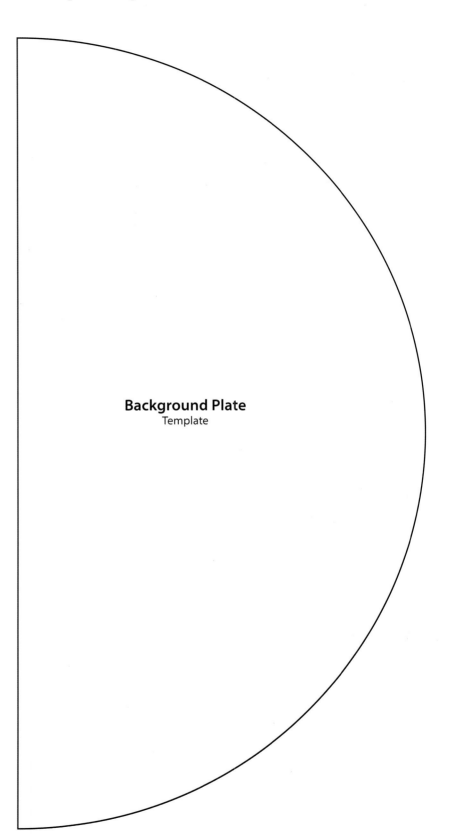

Background Plate
Template

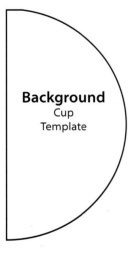

Background
Cup
Template

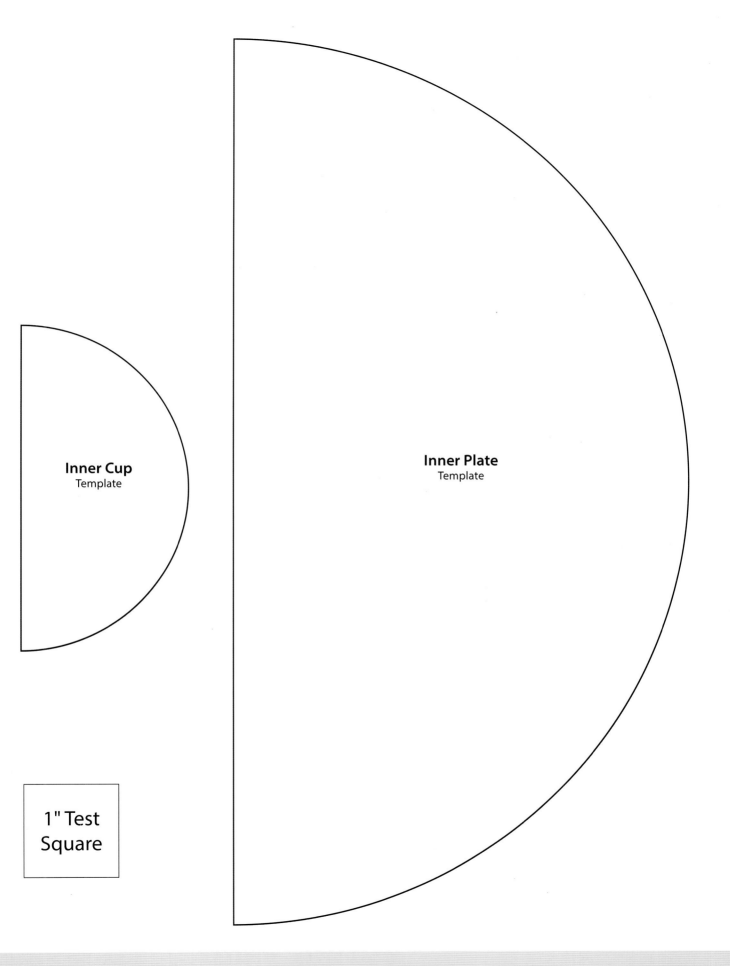

Inner Cup
Template

Inner Plate
Template

1" Test
Square

Book-Keeper Pillow

By Kiley Ferons of Kiley's Quilting Room

A pretty pillow offers comfort and support, as, of course, pillows do, but it has the added function of keeping your book or reader safe, sound, and exactly where you left it. The project works up so quickly, you'll be able to make one for all your little readers in their favorite fabrics and one for you, too! And what a perfect gift for all your book club friends.

MATERIALS NEEDED

- 18" (45.7cm) square pillow form
- Main front fabric: one 16½" x 16½" (41.9 x 41.9cm)
- Main back fabric: two 16½" x 20" (41.9 x 50.8cm)
- Accent front pocket fabric: one 16½" x 16½" (41.9 x 41.9cm)
- One 18" x 18" (45.7 x 45.7cm) piece of batting
- Rotary cutter
- Cutting mat
- Fabric scissors
- Fabric marking pen
- Needle
- Thread
- Pins or clips
- Quilting ruler

To make a pillow of a different size, get a square pillow form in the desired size and the following fabric sizes:
- **Main front fabric and accent front pocket fabric: 1½" (4cm) smaller than the pillow form**
- **Main back fabric: two pieces the same width as the main front fabric and 3"–5" (7.6–12.7cm) longer**
- **Batting: one piece in the same size as the pillow form**

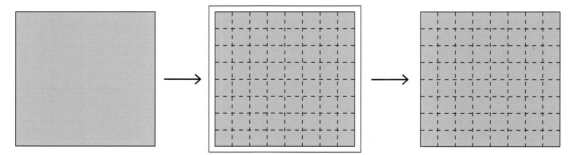

1. Lay the main front fabric piece on top of the batting and pin-baste in place. I like to stitch a line every 2" (5cm) or so and then turn and do the same in a perpendicular direction, creating a crosshatch pattern. Then trim off the excess batting.

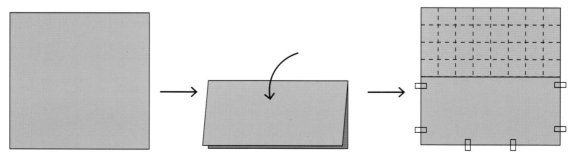

2. Fold the accent front pocket fabric in half, right side facing out. Place this on the bottom half of the main front fabric with the folded edge in the middle of the square and raw edges lined up. Pin or clip in place.

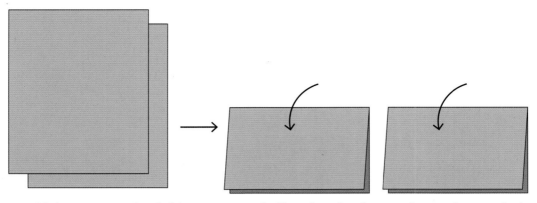

3. Fold the two main back fabric pieces in half so that the short ends match up with the short ends, right sides facing out.

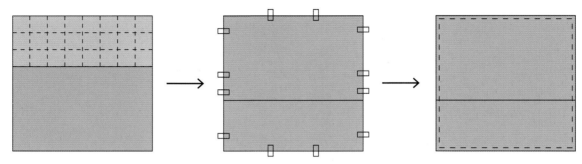

4. Place one of the folded main back fabric pieces on the bottom half of the square main front fabric and pocket, making sure that the raw edges are aligned and the folded edge is in the middle of the square. Do the same with the other folded main back fabric piece so that the folded edges overlap. Pin or clip in place and sew a ¼" (6mm) seam all the way around the square, catching all the layers as you go.

5. Flip the pillow cover right side out and insert the pillow form! Make sure that the pocket layer stays on the front of the pillow and the back pieces overlap around the back of the pillow insert.

6. Fill the pocket with books, bookmarks, treats, or whatever else you want. This is the perfect gift for an avid reader. I loved being able to choose fabrics that I knew matched each of my kids' personalities—or let them choose!

Work with a single color from the main pillow fabric to add a pocket that complements the overall look.

Rainbow Cotton Pottery

By Cindy Hilfiger of Cotton Pottery

We all have scraps from past quilting projects coming out our ears! Put those scraps to good use with this awesome and fun cotton pottery project. This is a great way to use up your scraps, use your knowledge of sewing, and try something new all at once!

MATERIALS NEEDED

- 13 FQ in chosen colors
- 100 ft. (30.5m) of ³⁄₁₆" (4.8cm) clothesline, also see Cutting Instructions to the right
- Glue stick
- Scrap paper
- Binding clip or clothespin
- Straight pins
- Scissors
- Sewing machine with zigzag stitch
- Thread of choice

CUTTING INSTRUCTIONS

Cut on the cross grain. Strips cut on the bias will pull and stretch, leaving little fabric coverage once wrapped on the clothesline. You don't need to cut the clothesline to length. You will need approximately 50 ft. (15.2m) to complete this but we recommend buying 100 ft. (30.5m) to be safe, as every bowl is slightly different in shape and size.

Fabrics	Cut Strips
First color	Seven ½" x 22" (1.5 x 55.9cm)
Next 11 colors	Four ½" x 22" (1.5 x 55.9cm) of each color
Last color (white or cream)	One ½" x 22" (1.5 x 55.9cm)

TIP

When wrapping the fabric on the clothesline, I find it easiest to stand or sit with the unwrapped clothesline under one foot while holding the other end with one hand and wrapping the fabric around the clothesline with the other hand. This helps you hold the clothesline taut while wrapping the fabric around it and helps prevent the tail of the fabric from getting tangled around the clothesline.

Wrapping the Clothesline

One strip of fabric measuring ½" x 22" (1.5 x 55.9cm) will wrap about 10"–12" (25.4–30.5cm) of clothesline. Wrap the strips of fabric on the clothesline in rainbow order. Use all strips of each color before moving to the next.

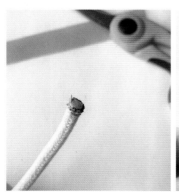 

1. If the end of the rope has been melted to prevent fraying, cut the melted end off before starting to wrap.

2. Grab your first strip of fabric, lay it on a piece of scrap paper, and run the glue stick over the first 3" (7.6cm) of one end. Don't forget to use your scrap paper each time you do this!

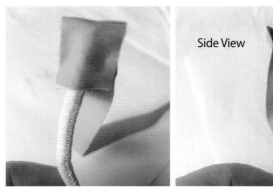

Side View

3. Take the glued end and wrap it over the end of your clothesline with about ½" (1.5cm) in the front, facing you, and the rest of the length of fabric on the back side.

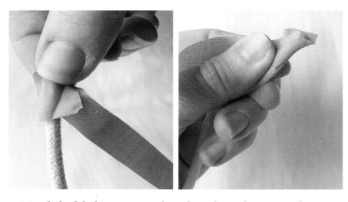

4. Pinch/hold the wrapped end and, with your other hand, grab the fabric tail in the back and bring it around to the front, as close to the end as you can get, overlapping the already-wrapped fabric in the front and completely covering the clothesline end.

5. After you've wrapped the long fabric tail all the way around the front, bring it to the back again and keep wrapping around, making sure that you overlap the previous layer each time.

6. When you get to the last 2" (5cm) of your first fabric strip, run the glue stick over the end of the wrong side of the fabric and then complete the wrap, place the binder clip over the end of the first strip to hold it in place while you prep the next strip.

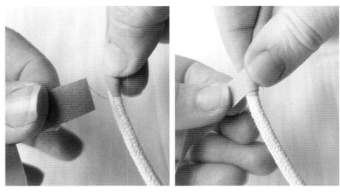

7. Grab the next strip, run the glue stick over the end, remove the binding clip, overlap the newly glued strip on top of the end of the last strip, and continue wrapping the new strip.

8. Keep wrapping in the same manner until you've used all but the last fabric strip.

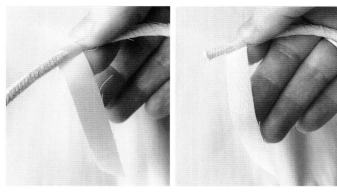

9. Start wrapping the last strip and when you get to the last 2" (5cm) of it, cut the clothesline so only 1" (2.5cm) of clothesline extends beyond what you have already wrapped.

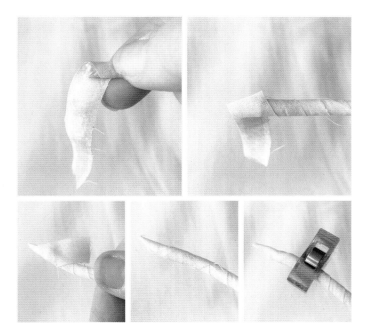

10. Run the glue stick over the 2" (5cm) end of the fabric strip and continue wrapping it on the last 1" (2.5cm) of clothesline. Continue wrapping the fabric on itself, past the end of the clothesline, to start making a point, and then start wrapping the strip back toward, and then past, the end of the clothesline. When you've finished wrapping, place the binder clip over the end of the strip to hold it in place until the glue dries.

These sewn bowls make great decorative storage for your sewing space or home. Once you know the technique, you can make a variety in different shapes, sizes, and colors to suit your needs.

Sewing the Cotton Pottery

1½" diameter

(Fiddlehead)

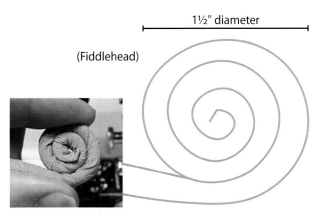

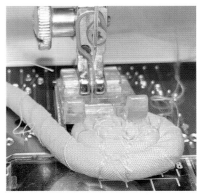

1. Grab the beginning of the clothesline (where you started wrapping) and make the shape of a fiddlehead by curling the clothesline into a flat spiral shape, as shown. Making sure your fiddlehead is tight, keep coiling it until it's about 1½" (4cm) in diameter. It may be tough to hold in a tight coil before you sew it; using pins in this step will help hold it in place.

3. Lift the presser foot, pull out the fiddlehead, and clip the thread. The fiddlehead should stay tightly coiled by itself now.

4. Set up the zigzag stitch on your sewing machine. I use 4.2 stitch width and 1.7 stitch length. Make sure your bobbin is full.

Start

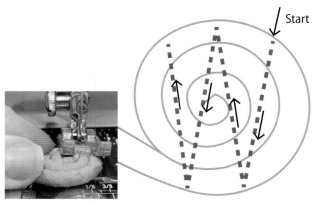

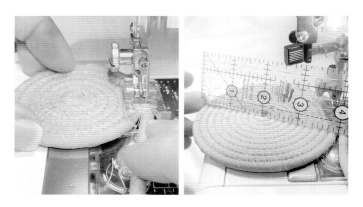

2. Go to your sewing machine, aka your "cotton potter's wheel." Place your fiddlehead under the foot of the sewing machine and straight-stitch a *W* onto it, starting with the right side of the *W* on the right-hand side of the fiddlehead as shown. Pull the pins as you sew.

5. Place your fiddlehead under the presser foot with the length of clothesline on the right-hand side. You will be stitching the last row of the fiddlehead to the next row of clothesline to create a base for the "pottery" bowl. Start your zigzag stitch near the outside of your stitched *W*. Keep sewing each new row to the last, making sure you are catching both sides with your zigzag stitch. Continue until your base is 4" (10cm) in diameter.

6. When you've reached a 4" (10cm) diameter, tip the base up as far as you can tip it and keep sewing around and around. You will see the sides of your bowl start to take shape. Keep the base of the bowl tipped at the same angle to create a bowl that gradually widens as it gets taller.

7. When you get to your last fabric strip, stop sewing and either back stitch or lock stitch to end your zigzag. Do not zigzag this last strip to the bowl. Lift the presser foot, pull out the bowl, and clip the thread.

The Finishing Touch

1. Make the cloud by bringing the remaining clothesline to the front of the bowl, creating the cloud shape, and using pins to hold the cloud in place.

2. Hand stitch or hot glue the cloud in place. If stitching, make sure that each stitch catches a part of the cloud, then plunges into the inside of the bowl and comes back out again until the entire cloud is stitched in place.

Scalloped Puff Quilt

By Kiley Ferons of Kiley's Quilting Room

No matter what era we are in, quilters are always looking to the past for inspiration. Puff quilts are not a new invention. They have been around for decades. But finding new and fun ways to create them is what makes them modern! This Scalloped Puff Quilt is made up of channels filled with stuffing and has scalloping at the edges. Be sure to check out the bias binding tutorial on page 164 to help make binding this quilt a lot easier!

MATERIALS NEEDED

- See Fabric Requirements below
- Polyfill
- Long dowel
- Rotary cutter
- Cutting mat
- Fabric scissors
- Fabric marking pen
- Needle
- Thread
- Pins
- Quilting ruler

Before You Start

- Read through all the instructions first.
- The size of the finished quilt is 58½" x 58½" (148.6 x 148.6cm).
- The WOF is assumed to be 42" (106.7cm).
- The seam allowance is ¼" (6mm) unless otherwise noted.
- Print the template at 100%, *not* "fit to page."
- When posting your quilt online or searching for ideas for your quilt, use or search the hashtag #ScallopedPuffQuilt.

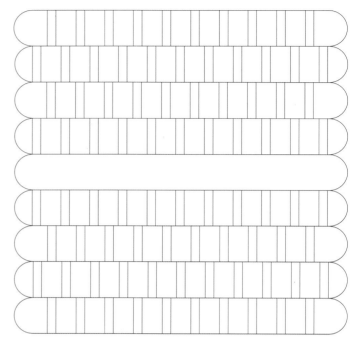

Copy and color in the black-and-white diagram to test different color arrangements before you cut!

FABRIC REQUIREMENTS AND CUTTING INSTRUCTIONS

Quilt Top				
Color 1	Color 2	Color 3	Color 4	Color 5
¾ yd. (68.6m)	1 yd. (90cm)	1 yd. (90cm)	1 yd. (90cm)	¾ yd. (68.6cm)
Two 7" (17.8cm) x WOF, sew end to end, Subcut: One 7" x 59" (17.8 x 149.9cm)	Four 7" (17.8cm) x WOF, Subcut: Twenty-four 7" x 4" (17.8 x 10cm) Twenty 7" x 2" (17.8 x 5cm)	Four 7" (17.8cm) x WOF, Subcut: Four 7" x 6½" (17.8 x 16.5cm) Eighteen 7" x 4" (17.8 x 10cm) Twenty-two 7" x 2" (17.8 x 5cm)	Four 7" (17.8cm) x WOF, Subcut: Twenty-four 7" x 4" (17.8 x 10cm) Twenty 7" x 2" (17.8 x 5cm)	Three 7" (17.8cm) x WOF, Subcut: Eighteen 7" x 4" (17.8 x 10cm) Four 7" x 6½" (17.8 x 16.5cm)
Two 2" (5cm) x WOF, Subcut: Twenty-two 7" x 2" (17.8 x 5cm)				
Backing	3¾ yds. (3.4m)			
Binding	½ yd. (45.7cm) to create bias binding			

Assembling the Rows

1. Take the 7" x 59" (17.8 x 149.9cm) Color 1 piece and place the scalloped edge template on one end, with the curve facing the short end as shown in the illustration, and cut along the curve. Do this to the other end as well. Label this as Row 1 and set it aside.

2. Starting with a Color 2 piece, alternate sewing 7" x 4" (17.8 x 10cm) Color 2 pieces (12 total) and 7" x 2" (17.8 x 5cm) Color 1 pieces (11 total), as shown in the illustration. Press the seams to one side. Follow the instructions from Step 1 to scallop the ends. Repeat this step to make another row and label them Row 2A and Row 2B.

3. Start with a 7" x 6½" (17.8 x 16.5cm) Color 3 piece, then alternate sewing 7" x 4" (17.8 x 10cm) Color 3 pieces (9 total) and 7" x 2" (17.8 x 5cm) Color 2 pieces (10 total), and end with another 7" x 6½" (17.8 x 16.5cm) Color 3 piece, as shown in the illustration. Press the seams to one side. Follow the instructions from Step 1 to scallop the ends. Repeat this step to make another row and label them Row 3A and Row 3B.

4. Starting with a Color 4 piece, alternate sewing 7"x 4" (17.8 x 10cm) Color 4 pieces (12 total) and 7"x 2" (17.8 x 5cm) Color 3 pieces (11 total), as shown in the illustration. Press the seams to one side. Follow the instructions from Step 1 to scallop the ends. Repeat this step to make another row and label them Row 4A and Row 4B.

5. Start with a 7" x 6½" (17.8 x 16.5cm) Color 5 piece, then alternate sewing 7"x 4" (17.8 x 10cm) Color 5 pieces (9 total) and 7"x 2" (17.8 x 5cm) Color 4 pieces (10 total), and end with another 7" x 6½" (17.8 x 16.5cm) Color 5 piece, as shown in the illustration. Press the seams to one side. Follow the instructions from Step 1 to scallop the ends. Repeat this step to make another row and label them Row 5A and Row 5B.

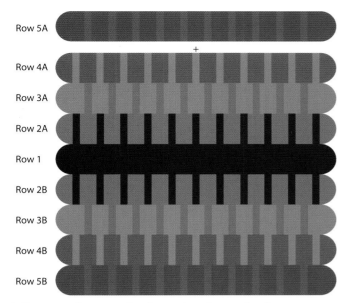

Row 5A
Row 4A
Row 3A
Row 2A
Row 1
Row 2B
Row 3B
Row 4B
Row 5B

6. Lay out the rows in the order shown in the illustration and sew them together.

Making the Puffs

1. Prepare the backing as needed and lay it down on a smooth, flat surface, right side down, and baste the quilt top onto it (no batting in between). You will quilt along the seam rows, so make sure you pin along those seams.

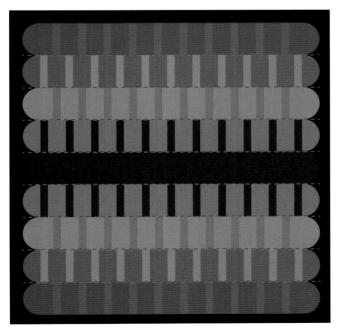

2. Quilt straight lines along the row seam lines, either in the "ditch" or just a hair to the side of it.

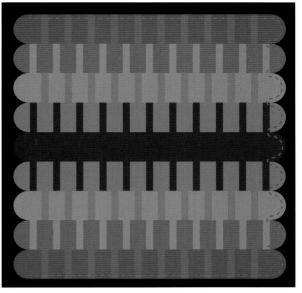

3. Stitch a scant ¼" (6mm) along the top, down one side, and along the bottom. Back stitch at the start and stop to keep the stitches holding firm. Keep the other side open so you can stuff the rows.

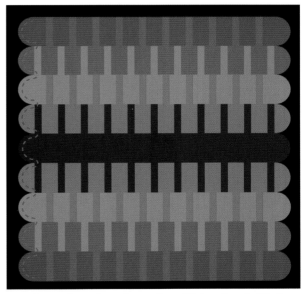

4. Use a long dowel to shove handfuls of polyfill down into each row. Fill as desired. Then stitch another scant ¼" (6mm) along the open side to close it. Trim off the excess backing.

5. Create the bias binding and bind your edges. It is important to use bias binding when going around curved edges because it stretches and molds better to the curves. You can find a detailed tutorial on how to make bias binding on page 164.

Template

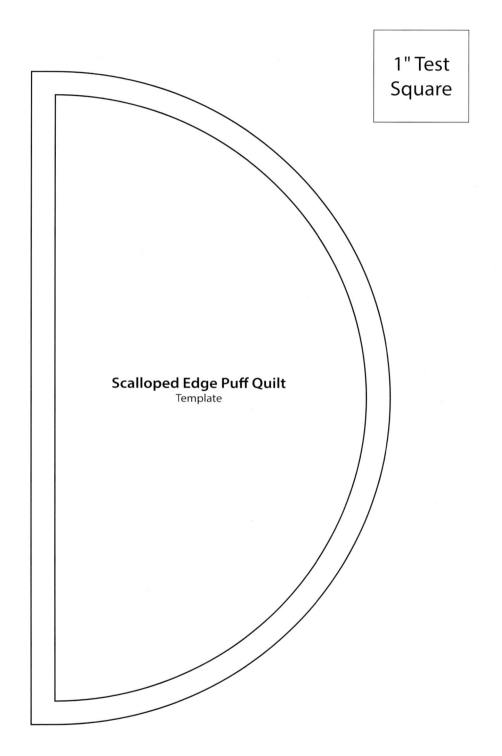

1" Test
Square

Scalloped Edge Puff Quilt
Template

III. Decor Quilts

When you spend hours of your time and
energy creating a work of art, you want to make
sure that people get the chance to enjoy it!
Don't display just your larger quilts—you can
make smaller quilts that are just as stunning for
displaying around your home. These quilts are
great for adding to your seasonal decor or
your everyday decor, and they don't take
up quite as much time and/or space as
some of your larger quilt projects.

The Friends of a Gourd project on page 46 is pieced in sections to create the perfect decorative wall hanging or table runner for fall.

Friends of a Gourd

By Kiley Ferons of Kiley's Quilting Room

There is nothing cozier than the combination of colder weather and quilts! This cute mini quilt is meant to show off your favorite fall colors all autumn long. You could even make two or three of these panels and sew them side to side to create a fun table runner. What would your ideal pumpkin patch look like?

MATERIALS NEEDED

- See Fabric Requirements below
- Rotary cutter
- Cutting mat
- Fabric scissors
- Fabric marking pen
- Needle
- Thread
- Pins
- Quilting ruler

Before You Start

- The finished size of the wall hanging is 28" x 12" (71.1 x 30.5cm).
- The seam allowance is ¼" (6mm) unless otherwise noted.
- Share your quilt on Instagram with the hashtag #FriendsOfAGourdQuilt.

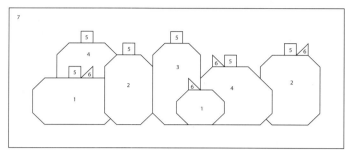

Copy and color in the black-and-white diagram to test different color arrangements before you cut!

FABRIC REQUIREMENTS

Tan plaid	One F8
Gold plaid	One F8
Gray	One F8
Blue	One F8
Black	One F8 or six 1½" x 1½" (4 x 4cm) scraps
Green	One F8 or four 1½" x 1½" (4 x 4cm) scraps
White	⅜ yd. (34.3cm)
Backing	One 32" x 16" (81.3 x 40.6cm) piece
Binding	¼ yd. (22.9m)

CUTTING INSTRUCTIONS

Tan plaid	One 4½" x 6½" (11.4 x 16.5cm) One 4½" x 3½" (11.4 x 8.9cm) One 1½" x 1½" (4 x 4cm)
Gold plaid	Two 4½" x 6½" (11.4 x 16.5cm) One 1½" x 2½" (4 x 6cm) Two 1½" x 1½" (4 x 4cm)
Gray	One 3½" x 4½" (8.9 x 11.4cm) One 3½" x 2½" (8.9 x 6cm) One 3½" x 1½" (8.9 x 4cm) Three 1½" x 1½" (4 x 4cm)
Blue	One 4½" x 4½" (11.4 x 11.4cm) One 2½" x 4½" (6 x 11.4cm) One 1½" x 3½" (4 x 8.9cm) Two 1½" x 2½" (4 x 6cm) Seven 1½" x 1½" (4 x 4cm)
Black	Six 1½" x 1½" (4 x 4cm)
Green	Four 1½" x 1½" (4 x 4cm)
White	Three 2½" (6cm) x WOF, Subcut: Two 2½" x 24½" (6 x 62.2cm) Two 2½" x 12½" (6 x 31.8cm) Two 2½" x 4½" (6 x 11.4cm) One 2½" x 2½" (6 x 6cm) Cut remaining strip to: 1½" (4cm) x WOF, Subcut: Twenty-one 1½" x 1½" (4 x 4cm) One 1½" (4cm) x WOF, Subcut: Four 1½" x 2" (4 x 5cm) Two 1½" x 2½" (4 x 6cm) Two 1½" x 4½" (4 x 11.4cm)

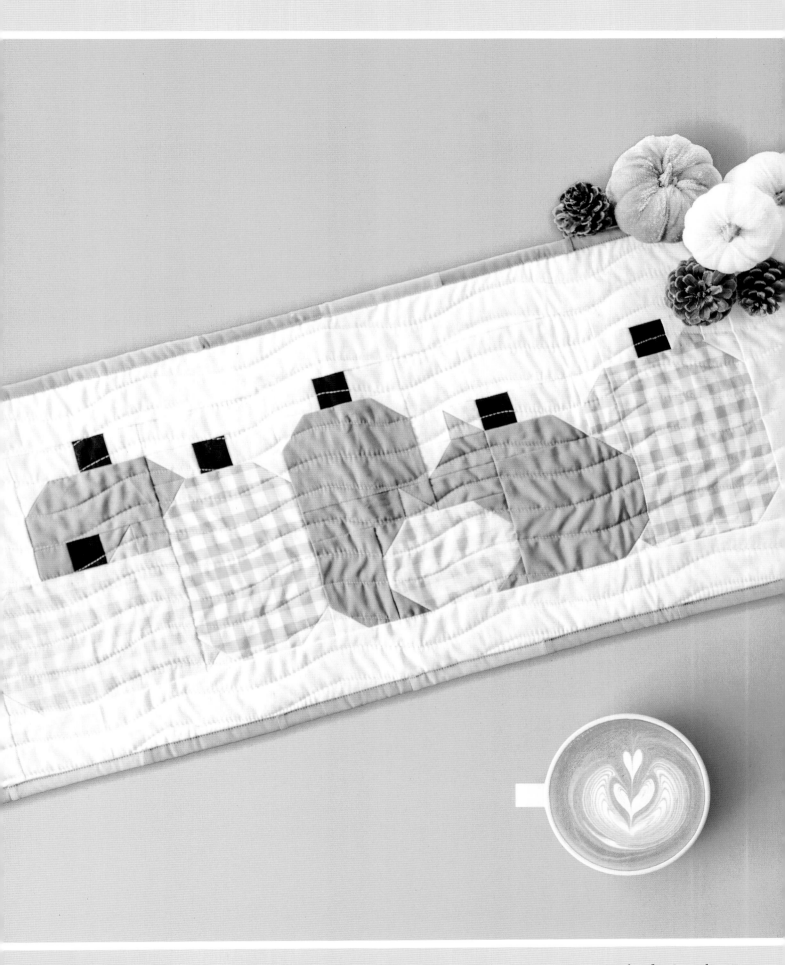

Section A

FABRIC PIECES NEEDED

Tan plaid	One 4½" x 6½" (11.4 x 16.5cm)
Blue	One 2½" x 4½" (6 x 11.4cm)
	Three 1½" x 1½" (4 x 4cm)
Black	Two 1½" x 1½" (4 x 4cm)
White	Five 1½" x 1½" (4 x 4cm)
	One 1½" x 2½" (4 x 6cm)
	One 1½" x 4½" (4 x 11.4cm)

1. Draw a diagonal line on the back of three 1½" (4cm) white squares and the 1½" (4cm) green square.

2. Row 1: Join together a white 1½" x 2½" (4 x 6cm) piece, a black square, and a white square. Press the seams to one side.

3. Row 2: Place a white square with a diagonal line, RST, in the upper left corner of the blue 4½" x 2½" (11.4 x 6cm) rectangle. Sew on the drawn line and trim the seam to ¼" (6mm). Press open.

4. Row 3: Place a 1½" (4cm) green square, RST, on a 1½" (4cm) blue square. Sew along the diagonal line and trim the seam to ¼" (6mm). Press open. Join together a blue square, a black square, the blue and green HST, and another blue square. Press the seams to one side.

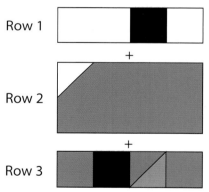

Row 1

+

Row 2

+

Row 3

5. Sew the rows together in order and press the seams.

Top Section

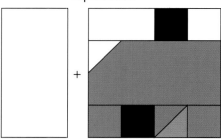

6. Sew the 2½" x 4½" (6 x 11.4cm) white piece to your blue pumpkin block. Press toward the white piece. This is the top section.

Bottom Section

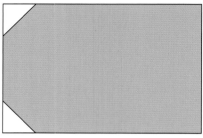

7. Add two of the white squares with a diagonal line, RST, to the left side corners of the tan plaid piece. Sew on the diagonal line. Trim the seam to ¼" (6mm) and press open. This is the bottom section.

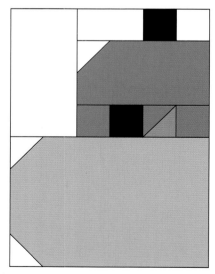

8. Sew the bottom section to the top section. Press the seams.

Section B

FABRIC PIECES NEEDED

Gold plaid	One 4½" x 6½" (11.4 x 16.5cm)
Tan plaid	One 1½" x 1½" (4 x 4cm)
Black	One 1½" x 1½" (4 x 4cm)
Blue	Two 1½" x 1½" (4 x 4cm)
White	Three 1½" x 1½" (4 x 4cm) Two 1½" x 2" (4 x 5cm) One 1½" x 4½" (4 x 11.4cm)

HST

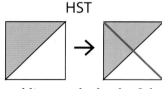

1. Draw a diagonal line on the back of three 1½" (4cm) white squares and two 1½" (4cm) blue squares. Make one HST with one of the 1½" (4cm) white squares and a tan plaid square, RST. Press and trim the seams. Draw another diagonal line on the back of this HST.

2. Row 2: Lay a blue square on the left end of a 1½" x 2" (4 x 5cm) white piece, RST, with the diagonal line starting at the top corner.

3. Sew along the diagonal line. Press open and trim. Add a 1½" (4cm) black square, then add another 1½" x 2" (4 x 5cm) white piece.

Top Section

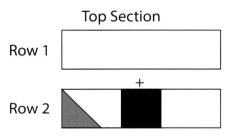

Row 1

+

Row 2

4. Row 1: Add to Row 2 as shown. Press the seams. This is the top section.

Bottom Section

5. Add a 1½" (4cm) blue square to the top left corner of the gold plaid piece; add a 1½" (4cm) white square to both corners on the right; and add the previously made white and tan HST to the bottom left corner. Press the seams and trim the excess. This is the bottom section.

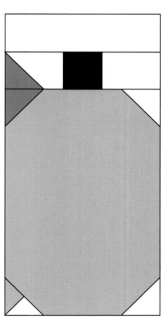

6. Sew the top section to the bottom section. Press the seams.

Section C

FABRIC PIECES NEEDED

Tan plaid	One 3½" x 4½" (8.9 x 11.4cm)
Gray	One 3½" x 4½" (8.9 x 11.4cm) One 3½" x 1½" (8.9 x 4cm) Three 1½" x 1½" (4 x 4cm) One 2½" x 3½" (6 x 8.9cm)
Black	One 1½" x 1½" (4 x 4cm)
Blue	Two 1½" x 2½" (4 x 6cm) Two 1½" x 1½" (4 x 4cm)
Green	Two 1½" x 1½" (4 x 4cm)
White	Six 1½" x 1½" (4 x 4cm) Two 1½" x 2" (4 x 5cm) One 2½" x 2½" (6 x 6cm)

1. Draw a diagonal line on the back of five 1½" (4cm) white squares, three 1½" (4cm) gray squares, and two 1½" (4cm) blue squares.

HST

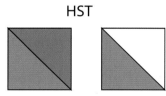

2. Make two HSTs: one with a green and a gray square and one with a green and a white square. Be sure that they are in the correct positions when assembling. Press and trim.

3. Row 1: Sew a 1½" x 2" (4 x 5cm) white piece to a 1½" (4cm) black square. Sew another 1½" x 2" (4 x 5cm) white piece to the other side of the black square. Press the seams.

4. Row 2: Place two white squares with a diagonal line on both top corners of the 3½" x 4½" (8.9 x 11.4cm) gray piece. Press and trim.

Top Left Section

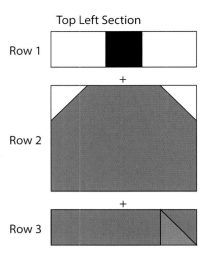

Row 1

Row 2

Row 3

5. Row 3: Sew the green and gray HST to the right end of the 3½" x 1½" (8.9 x 4cm) gray piece. Press the seams. Sew the rows together and press the seams. This is the top left section.

6. Row 2: Sew the 1½" (4cm) white square that has no diagonal line on it to the green and white HST. Press the seams.

Top Right Section

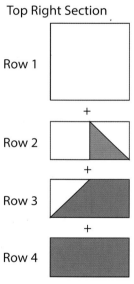

Row 1

Row 2

Row 3

Row 4

7. Row 3: Add a 1½" (4cm) white square with a diagonal line to the left side of a 1½" x 2½" (4 x 6cm) blue piece. Press open and trim the excess. Add the rows together, starting with the 2½" x 2½" (6 x 6cm) white piece (Row 1) and ending with the 1½" x 2½" (4 x 6cm) blue piece (Row 4). This is the top right section.

8. Take the 3½" x 4½" (8.9 x 11.4cm) tan plaid piece and add a gray square to both of the left-side corners, RST, sewing on the diagonal line. Then add a blue square to both of the right-side corners, RST, sewing on the diagonal line. Press the seams and trim the excess.

Bottom Section

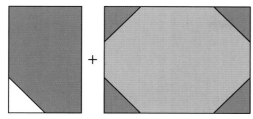

9. Add a white square to the bottom left corner of the 2½" x 3½" (6 x 8.9cm) gray piece. Sew on the diagonal. Press open, trim the excess, and then sew this block to the left side of the tan plaid block. Press the seams.

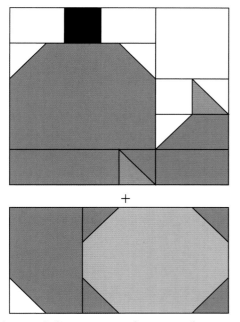

10. Sew the top left section to the top right section. Press the seam, then add the bottom section. Press the seams.

Section D

FABRIC PIECES NEEDED

Blue	One 4½" x 4½" (11.4 x 11.4cm) One 1½" x 3½" (4 x 8.9cm)
Gold plaid	Two 1½" x 1½" (4 x 4cm) One 1½" x 2½" (4 x 6cm)
Black	One 1½" x 1½" (4 x 4cm)
White	Three 1½" x 1½" (4 x 4cm) One 1½" x 2½" (4 x 4cm) One 2½" x 4½" (6 x 11.4cm)

1. Take three 1½" (4cm) white squares and one 1½" (4cm) gold plaid square and draw a diagonal line on the backs.

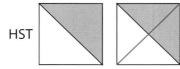

HST

2. Create your first HST by adding a white square with a diagonal line on it to a gold plaid piece. Sew on the diagonal line. Press and trim the excess. Draw another diagonal line, perpendicular to the seam you just created, on the back of this HST.

3. Row 1: Sew a 1½" x 2. ½" (4 x 6cm) white piece to the right side of a 1½" (4cm) black square.

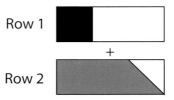

Row 1

Row 2

4. Row 2: Add a 1½" (4cm) white square with a diagonal line on it to the right side of the 1½" x 3½" (4 x 8.9cm) blue piece. Sew on the diagonal line. Press and trim the excess. Sew the rows together and press the seams.

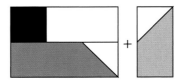

5. Add a 1½" (4cm) white square with a diagonal line on it to the top of a 1½"x 2½" (4 x 6cm) gold plaid piece. Sew on the diagonal line. Press and trim the excess. Add this piece to the right side of the top section. Press the seams.

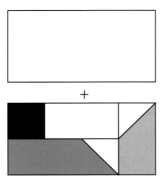

6. Add the 2½" x 4½" (6 x 11.4cm) white piece to the top of the top section. Press the seams.

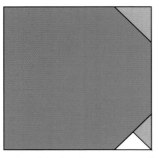

7. Add a 1½" (4cm) gold plaid square with a diagonal line to the top right corner of the 4½" (11.4cm) blue square. Sew on the diagonal line. Press and trim the excess. Next, take the previously made white and gold HST and add it to the bottom right corner of the blue square. Sew on the diagonal line. Press and trim.

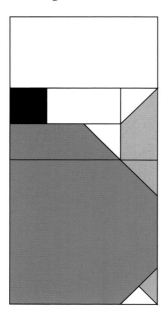

8. Sew the bottom section to the top section. Press the seams.

Section E

FABRIC PIECES NEEDED

Gold plaid	One 4½" x 6½" (11.4 x 16.5cm)
Black	One 1½" x 1½" (4 x 4cm)
Green	One 1½" x 1½" (4 x 4cm)
White	Five 1½" x 1½" (4 x 4cm) One 1½" x 4½" (4 x 11.4cm)

Top Section

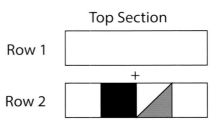

1. Row 2: Sew a 1½" (4cm) white square to a 1½" (4cm) black square, then add a white and green HST. Next, add another 1½" (4cm) white square. Sew Row 1 (the 1½" x 4½" [4 x 11.4cm] white piece) to the top of Row 2. This is the top section.

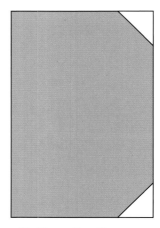

Bottom Section

2. Add a 1½" (4cm) white square to the right top and right bottom corners of the 4½" x 6½" (11.4 x 16.5cm) gold piece. Sew on the diagonal. Press the seam and trim the excess. This is the bottom section. Sew the bottom and top sections together. Press the seams.

Hang this piece on the wall or place it on a tabletop and arrange small gourds, pine cones, and other fall decorations to create the perfect decor centerpiece.

Assembling the Sections

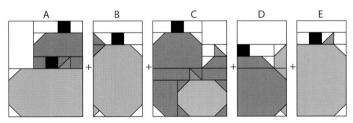

1. Sew the completed sections together as shown in the illustration.

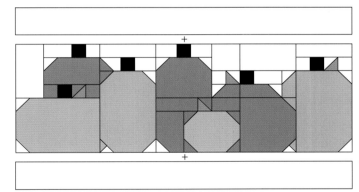

2. Add the 2½" x 24½" (6 x 62.2cm) white pieces to the top and bottom of the pumpkins. Press the seams.

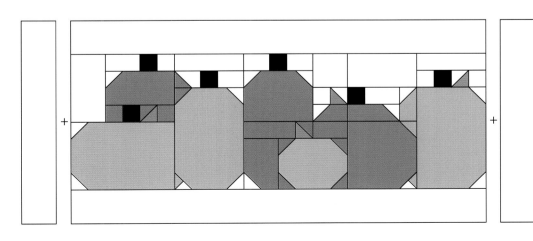

3. Sew the 2½" x 12½" (6 x 31.8cm) white pieces to the ends. Press the seams.

Infinity Mini

By Erin Grogan of Love Sew Modern

Hand sewing, especially English paper piecing (EPP), takes a lot of time and patience. This pattern is a smaller EPP project to give you a taste of hand piecing. It's a beautiful and modern design that is sure to impress anyone who sees your work!

MATERIALS NEEDED

- See Fabric Requirements below
- Sewline glue pen
- Card stock
- 80wt or 100wt thread
- Milliners needles, size 10
- Scissors
- Marking pen

Before You Start

- The finished quilt size is 23¾" x 23¾" (60.3 x 60.3cm).
- Be sure to print the templates at 100%.
- Share your quilt on Instagram using the hashtag #InfinityMiniEPP.

Fabric Requirements

Approximately 1 FQ per color. With paper piecing, you cut your fabric as you work, making it difficult to precisely estimate how much fabric you will need.

Cutting Instructions

Print the templates on page 58 on card stock and cut them out directly on the lines. Cut the following amounts of fabric pieces ¼"–⅜" (6–10mm) larger than the paper templates.

Template 1 Color A	Template 2 Color B	Template 2 Color C	Template 2 Color D	Template 3 Color C	Template 4 Color E	Template 5 Color E
Qty x 12	x 20	x 12	x 8	x 4	x 16	x 8

Copy and color in the black-and-white diagram to test different color arrangements before you cut!

Template Basting

BASTING TIPS

- Before glue-basting, snip into the fabric's seam allowance around curves as shown in the step diagrams.
- Baste your pieces the same way each time to help them nest together easily.
- When glue-basting, do not get glue on the edges of your templates. If you do, your needle will get covered in glue and become difficult to use.

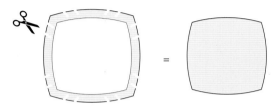

1. For Template 1, fold down the top and bottom edges first, then fold down the sides.

2. For Templates 2 and 3, fold down the top corner and bottom edge first, then fold down the sides.

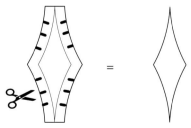

3. For Template 4, fold down all of the left side, then all of the right side. Don't fold down the top or the bottom.

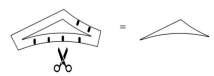

4. For Template 5, fold down the bottom edge first, then fold down the sides.

Assembly Instructions

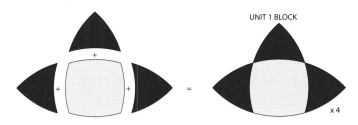

UNIT 1 BLOCK

x 4

1. Using four Color A Template 1 pieces and twelve Color B Template 2 pieces, assemble four Unit 1 blocks.

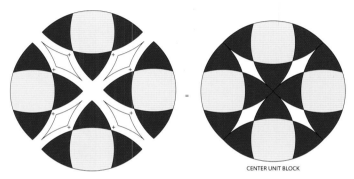

CENTER UNIT BLOCK

2. Join the four completed units using four Color E Template 4 pieces as shown in the diagram.

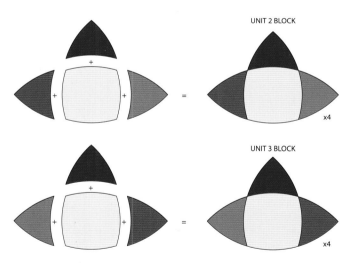

UNIT 2 BLOCK

x4

UNIT 3 BLOCK

x4

3. Using eight Color A Template 1 pieces, eight Color B Template 2 pieces, eight Color C Template 2 pieces, and eight Color D Template 2 pieces, assemble four Unit 2 blocks and four Unit 3 blocks.

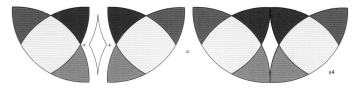

4. Pair each Unit 2 block with a Unit 3 block using a Color E Template 4 piece. Be sure to join them with the Color D Template 2 pieces touching, as shown.

8. Sew a Color E Template 5 piece onto both sides of a Color C Template 3 piece. Make four of these Unit 4 blocks.

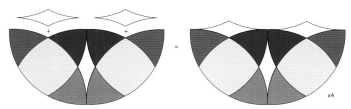

5. Sew two Color E Template 4 pieces onto all four completed units as shown in the diagram.

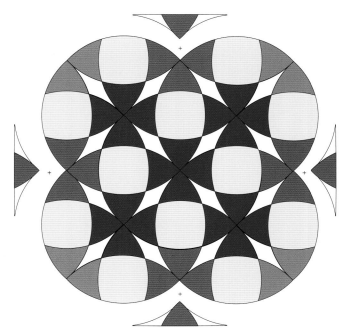

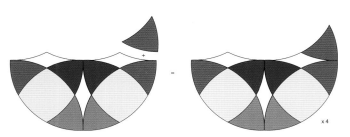

6. Sew a Color C Template 2 piece onto the top right of the four completed units as shown in the diagram.

9. Finish by sewing the Unit 4 blocks onto the completed unit as shown in the diagram.

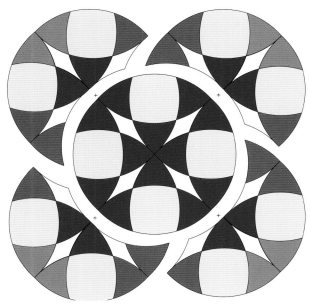

7. Sew the completed units onto the center unit block as shown in the diagram.

Templates

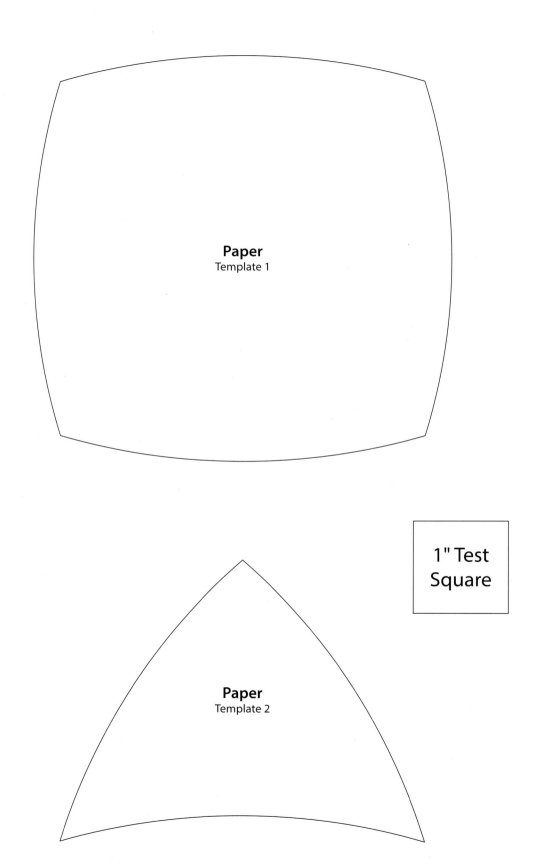

Paper
Template 1

1" Test
Square

Paper
Template 2

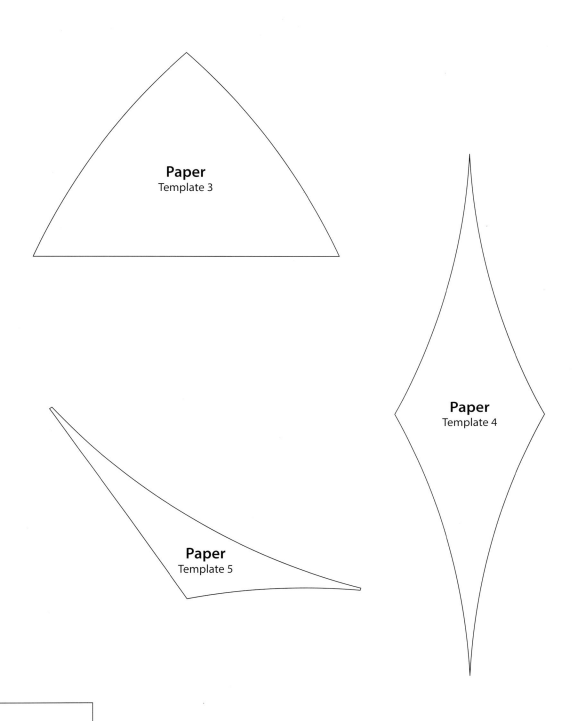

Paper
Template 3

Paper
Template 4

Paper
Template 5

1" Test
Square

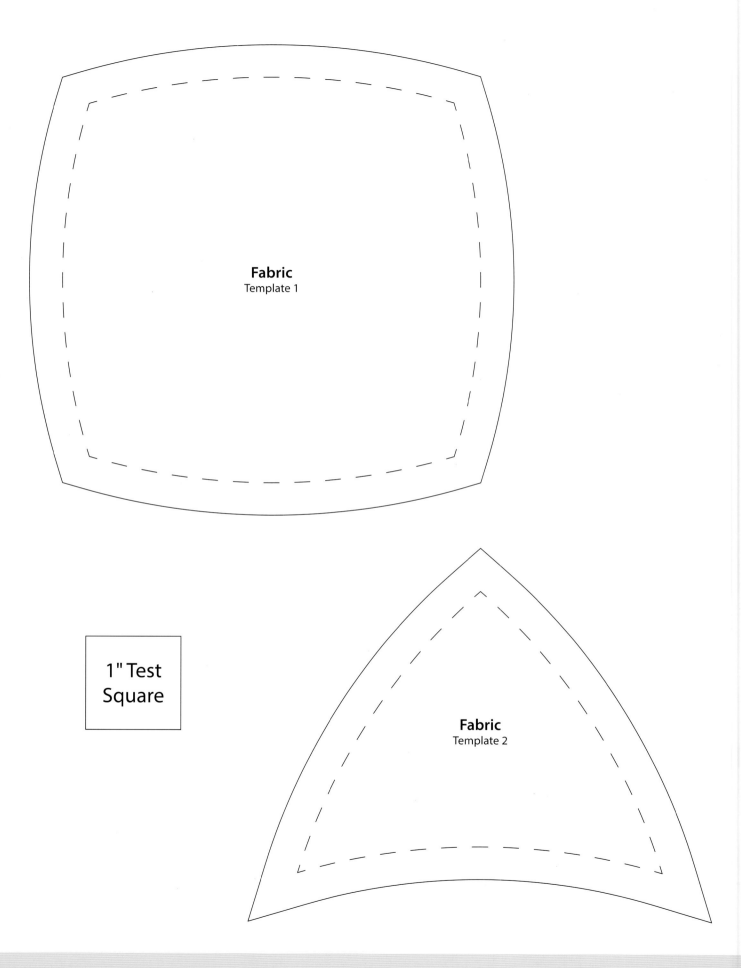

Fabric
Template 1

1" Test
Square

Fabric
Template 2

1" Test
Square

Fabric
Template 3

Fabric
Template 4

Fabric
Template 5

Metztli

By Jess Poémape

This quilt was inspired by Kiley's original quilt pattern, Citlali (see-TLAH-lee). The original quilt pattern requires hundreds of small HSTs, which can be intimidating for many quilters! To make this pattern more approachable, Jess blew up a single block by more than 400 percent for the baby size and 1600 percent for the throw size. The blocks are designed to be oversized so that they can be trimmed down, which will help keep all your stars on point when sewing together the top. She hopes that this version is more accessible for the everyday quilter.

The name for the original pattern, Citlali, is a Nahuatl word that means "star." To stay within the theme, Jess decided to name this quilt Metztli (METST-lee), a Nahuatl name for the goddess of the night or moon.

MATERIALS NEEDED

- See Fabric Requirements below
- Rotary cutter
- Cutting mat
- Fabric scissors
- Fabric marking pen
- Needle
- Thread
- Pins
- Quilting ruler
- Batting

Before You Start

- Read all the instructions first.
- The WOF is assumed to be 42" (106.7cm).
- The seam allowance is ¼" (6mm) unless otherwise noted.

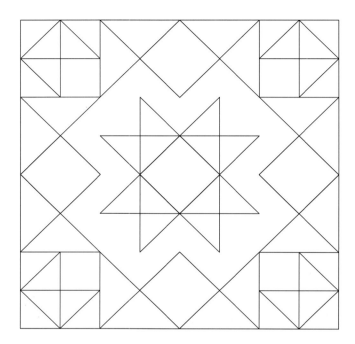

FABRIC REQUIREMENTS

	Baby 40" x 40" (101.6 x 101.6cm)	Throw 64" x 64" (162.6 x 162.6cm)
Color A	¼ yd. (22.9cm)	⅓ yd. (30.5cm)
Color B	⅔ yd. (61cm)	1 yd. (90cm)
Color C	¼ yd. (22.9cm)	⅔ yd. (61cm)
Color D	¾ yd. (68.6cm)	⅔ yd. (61cm)
Background	1½ yds. (1.4m)	2½ yds. (2.3m)
Backing	2½ yds. (2.3m)	4 yds. (3.7m)
Binding	⅜ yd. (34.3cm)	½ yd. (45.7cm)

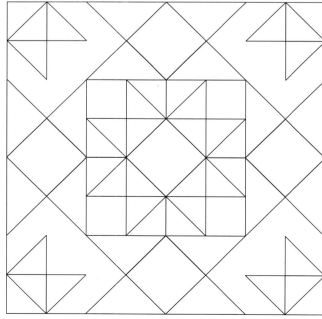

Copy and color in the black-and-white diagram to test different color arrangements before you cut!

CUTTING INSTRUCTIONS

	Baby 40" x 40" (101.6 x 101.8cm)	Throw 64" x 64" (162.6 x 162.6cm)
Color A	One 6¼" (15.9cm) x WOF strip, Subcut: Four 6¼" (15.9cm) squares (Label A1)	One 9¼" (23.5cm) x WOF strip, Subcut: Four 9¼" (23.5cm) squares (Label A1)
Color B	One 12" (30.5cm) x WOF strip, Subcut: Two 12" (30.5cm) squares (Label B1)	One 18" (45.7cm) x WOF strip, Subcut: Two 18" (45.7cm) squares (Label B1)
	One 6¼" (15.9cm) x WOF strip, Subcut: Two 6¼" (15.9cm) squares (Label B2)	One 9¼" (23.5cm) x WOF strip, Subcut: Two 9¼" (23.5cm) squares (Label B2)
Color C	One 6¼" (15.9cm) x WOF strip, Subcut: Six 6¼" (15.9cm) squares (Label C1)	Two 9¼" (23.5cm) x WOF strips, Subcut: Six 9¼" (23.5cm) squares (Label C1)
Color D	One 12" (30.5cm) x WOF strip, Subcut: Two 12" (30.5cm) squares (Label D1)	One 18" (45.7cm) x WOF strip, Subcut: Two 18" (45.7cm) squares (Label D1)
Background	Two 12" (30.5cm) x WOF strips, Subcut: Four 12" (30.5cm) squares (Label BG1)	Two 18" (45.7cm) x WOF strips, Subcut: Four 18" (45.7cm) squares (Label BG1)
	Two 6¼" (15.9cm) x WOF strips, Subcut: Twelve 6¼" (15.9cm) squares (Label BG2)	Three 9¼" (23.5cm) x WOF strips, Subcut: Twelve 9¼" (23.5cm) squares (Label BG2)
	Two 5½" (14cm) x WOF strips, Subcut: Eight 5½" (14cm) squares (Label BG3)	Two 8½" (21.6cm) x WOF strips, Subcut: Eight 8½" (21.6cm) squares (Label BG3)
Binding	Five 2½" (6cm) x WOF strips	Seven 2½" (6cm) x WOF strips

You can achieve either look shown depending on how you rotate the blocks.

Hourglass Block Construction: Three-Color Hourglass Blocks

1. To make four identical hourglass blocks, you will need two BG1 squares, one B1 square, and one D1 square.

2. Pair one BG1 square with one B1 square.

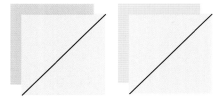

3. Use a pencil to draw a diagonal line from one corner to the other corner on the wrong side of the BG1 square.

4. With RST, stitch a ¼" (6mm) seam away from both sides of the marked line.

5. Using a rotary cutter, cut the squares apart on the marked diagonal line, making two HSTs. Press the seams open.

6. Repeat Steps 2–5 with the D1 square and the remaining BG1 square. You should now have four HSTs.

7. Place one HST in Color B and one HST in Color D RST, making sure the colors are opposite each other.

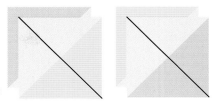

8. On the top HST, draw a diagonal line corner to corner, perpendicular to the seam. Pin the center intersection of the hourglass to make sure the points will match up.

9. Stitch a ¼" (6mm) seam away from both sides of the marked line.

10. Using a rotary cutter, cut the squares apart on the marked diagonal line, making two hourglass blocks. Press the seam open. Trim each to 10½" (26.7cm) square for a baby blanket or 16½" (41.9cm) square for a throw.

11. Repeat with the other set of HSTs. You should have four hourglass blocks.

12. Repeat with the remaining BG1, B1, and D1 pieces. Make eight hourglass blocks total.

HST Block Construction: Two-at-a-Time HSTs

1. To make two HSTs, place one BG2 square RST with one A1 square. Pin in place.

2. Draw a diagonal line on the back of one square.

3. Sew ¼" (6mm) away from both sides of the drawn line.

4. Cut along the drawn line.

5. Open the HSTs and press the seams open. You should end up with two identical HSTs. Trim each to 5½" (14cm) square for a baby blanket or 8½" (21.6cm) square for a throw.

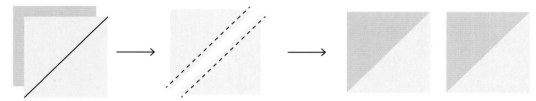

6. Repeat Steps 1–5 for the remaining A1, B2, and C1 pieces paired with BG2 squares.

Quilt Top Assembly

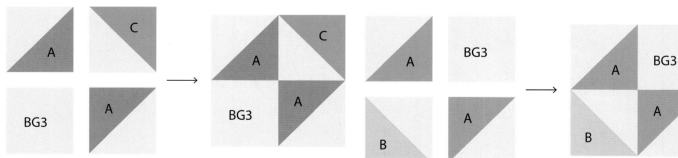

1. Make a Unit 1 set using one BG3 square, one HST in Color C, and two HSTs in Color A. Press the seams open.

2. Make a Unit 2 set using one BG3 square, one HST in color B, and two HSTs in color C. Press the seams open.

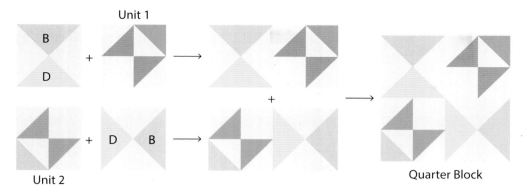

Unit 1

Unit 2

Quarter Block

3. Make a quarter block by sewing together a Unit 1 set, a Unit 2 set, and two hourglass blocks. Refer to the diagram for color placement. Press the seams open.

4. Sew four quarter blocks together to assemble the quilt top. Press the seams open.

Option 1

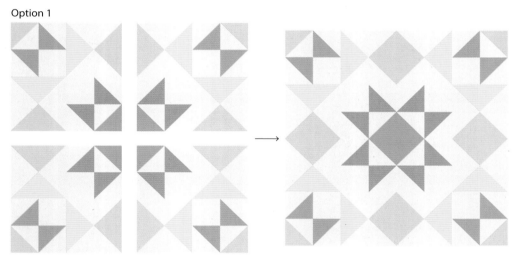

- Option 1: Rotate the quarter blocks so the Color C HSTs meet in the center.

Option 2

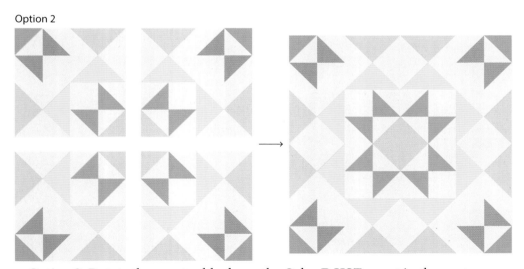

- Option 2: Rotate the quarter blocks so the Color B HSTs meet in the center.

5. Piece the backing together for the desired quilt size. Baste, quilt, and bind. Enjoy!

Potted Minis

By Kiley Ferons of Kiley's Quilting Room

Not everyone is blessed with a green thumb or has the space for living plants. These Potted Mini patterns are a great way to bring greenery and fresh inspiration into your space. There are two size options to suit your needs—or you can make both!

MATERIALS NEEDED

- See Fabric Requirements (page 70)
- Rotary cutter
- Cutting mat
- Fabric scissors
- Fabric marking pen
- Needle
- Thread
- Pins
- Quilting ruler
- Batting

Copy and color in the black-and-white diagrams to test different color arrangements before you cut!

Before You Start

- The instructions are written for the small Potted Mini, but the steps are the same for the regular Potted Mini unless otherwise noted.

- This pattern is written with both a reverse appliqué technique and a raw-edge appliqué technique. Read through both before choosing and getting started.

- Regardless of which technique you choose, you will need to print the templates. Be sure to print them at 100 percent, not "fit to page." Measure the 1" (2.5cm) reference square on your printout to ensure that everything is the correct size.

- You will need a washable glue stick for either technique.

- If you are using two layers for the background, lay them on top of each other on a cutting mat so that the edges all line up. If you are using only one layer, lay it out on the cutting mat.

- **For the small Potted Mini only:** Using the curve guide, line up each end of the guideline with the side and bottom of the 16" x 26" (40.6 x 66cm) background piece(s). Cut along the curve. Do this to both bottom corners of the background piece(s).

- Share this quilt on Instagram using the hashtag #PottedMiniQuilt.

FABRIC REQUIREMENTS AND CUTTING INSTRUCTIONS

	Small Potted Mini	Potted Mini
Background	½ yd. (45.7cm)	1 yd. (90cm)
	One 16" x 26" (40.6 x 66cm)	One 32" x 32" (81.3 x 81.3cm)
Pots	One 5" x 5" (12.7 x 12.7cm)	1 FQ
Leaves	½ yd. (45.7cm) or twelve 4" x 5" (10 x 12.7cm) scraps	3 FQs
Backing	One 20" x 30" (50.8 x 76.2cm)	One 36" x 36" (91.4 x 91.4cm)
Binding	100" (254cm) of bias binding	¼ yd. (22.9cm)
		Four 2½" (6cm) x WOF

This design is perfect for mixing modern touches with rustic charm in those smaller, odd-to-decorate spaces in your home.

Reverse Appliqué Technique

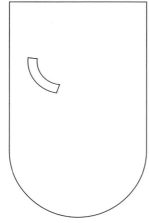

1. Lay the pot template(s) on top of the background piece where you want it positioned and trace it using washable ink or a marking tool (such as a hera marker).

2. Place and trace the leaf template(s). We made twelve pothos leaves for the small Potted Mini and fourteen for the regular Potted Mini. We also made three *Monstera* leaves for the regular Potted Mini. You can add or remove any number of leaves until it looks the way you want it.

3. Cut out the shapes you have traced on the background fabric. Start in the center of each shape with a snip and then make your way to the outline and cut very carefully along the marked lines.

TIP

If you are using a double-layered background, you may want to glue-baste the two pieces of fabric together so they don't shift while you are cutting through the layers.

4. Lay the background piece face down on a surface and arrange your pot(s) and leaves face down where you want them. Trim the pieces to fit the shapes if needed so that they don't show through on the wrong cutout (for example, you don't want the pot fabric to show through in one of the leaf cutouts). Glue-baste your pieces in place around the edges of the fabric pieces.

5. Place the piece of batting on top of the face-down layers, followed by your backing. Carefully flip the assembly over so it's face up. Use basting pins to stabilize everything.

6. Carefully hand- or machine-stitch around each cutout (options include a very small zigzag stitch or a blanket stitch); about ⅛"–¼" (3–6mm) away from the edges. Continue to quilt as desired, then bind using a bias binding. (See page 164.)

Regular Appliqué Technique

1. Lay the pot template(s) on the back of the pot fabric, trace around it, then cut it out, being careful to stay on the lines. Do the same with the leaf template(s), making about twelve leaves. We made twelve pothos leaves for the small Potted Mini and fourteen for the regular Potted Mini. We also made three Monstera leaves for the regular Potted Mini. You can add or remove any number of leaves until it looks the way you want it.

2. Arrange the cut-out fabric pieces on top of the background piece. When you like the way they are arranged, glue-baste them in place.

3. Place the piece of batting and backing behind the background piece. Use basting pins to stabilize everything.

EXTRA SMALL POTTED MINI

4. Carefully hand- or machine-stitch around each cut piece (options include a very small zigzag stitch or a blanket stitch), about ⅛"–¼" (3–6mm) in from the edges. Continue to quilt as desired, then bind using a bias binding. (See page 164.)

Templates

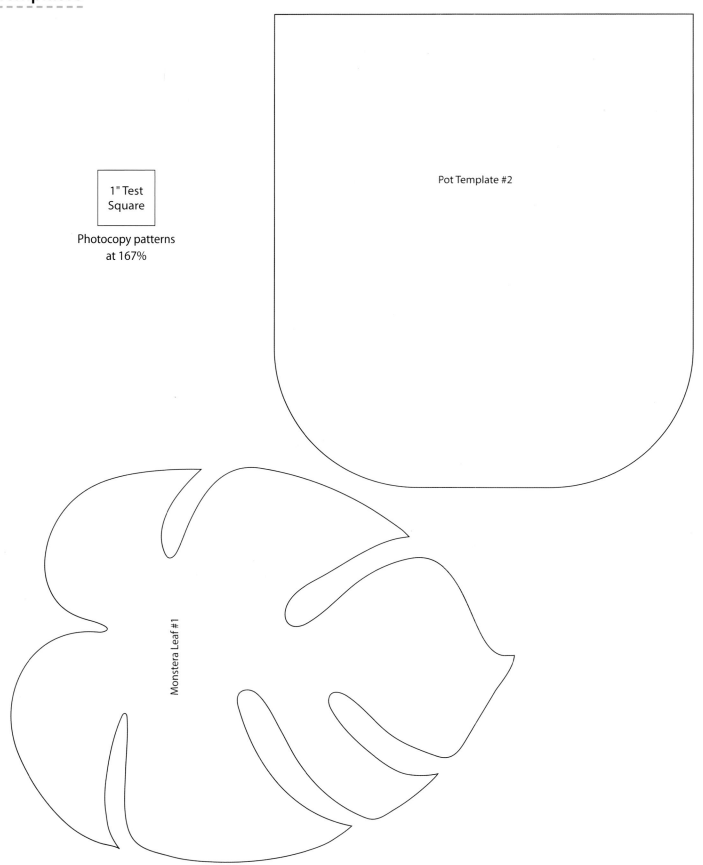

1" Test
Square

Photocopy patterns
at 167%

Pot Template #2

Monstera Leaf #1

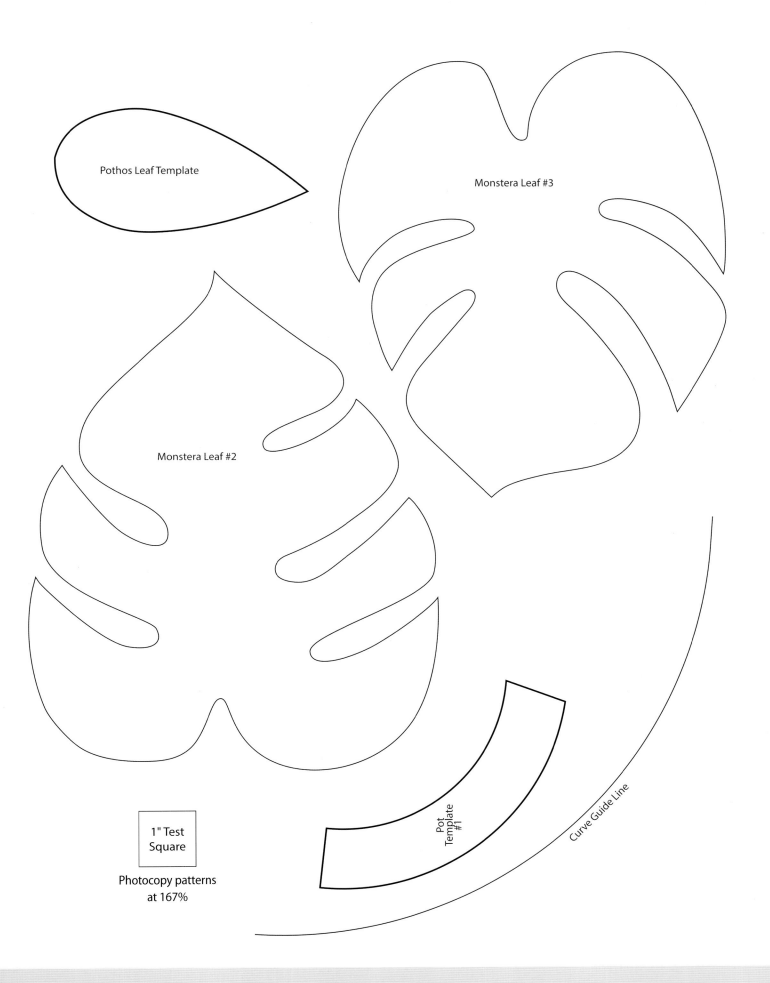

Pothos Leaf Template

Monstera Leaf #3

Monstera Leaf #2

1" Test
Square

Photocopy patterns
at 167%

Pot
Template
#1

Curve Guide Line

Totally Rad Mini

By Kiley Ferons of Kiley's Quilting Room

The peace sign has always been a symbol of happiness, love, and acceptance. This mini is a great way to add some of that positive energy into your home while also learning some new techniques. This pattern combines curves, Y-seams, and traditional piecing methods in a small and manageable way.

MATERIALS NEEDED

- See Fabric Requirements below
- Rotary cutter
- Cutting mat
- Fabric scissors
- Fabric marking pen
- Needle
- Thread
- Pins
- Quilting ruler
- Batting

Before You Start

- Read through all the instructions first.
- The finished size of the quilt is 20" x 40" (50.8 x 101.6cm).
- The WOF is assumed to be 42" (106.7cm).
- The binding is assumed to be 2½" (6cm) wide.
- The seam allowance is ¼" (6mm) unless otherwise noted.
- Print the templates at 100 percent, not "fit to page." Measure the 1" (2.5cm) reference square on your printout to ensure that everything is the correct size.
- When posting online or searching for ideas for your quilt, use or search the hashtag #TotallyRadMiniQuilt.

FABRIC REQUIREMENTS AND CUTTING INSTRUCTIONS

Color 1	1 FQ	One 2½" x 17½" (6 x 44.5cm) One 2½" x 19½" (6 x 49.5cm) One 7" x 10" (17.8 x 25.4cm) cutout using the peace sign section template
Color 2	1 FQ	Two 2½" x 20½" (6 x 52.1cm) One 2½" x 16½" (6 x 41.9cm) One 7" x 10" (17.8 x 25.4cm) cutout using the peace sign section template
Color 3	1 FQ	One 2½" x 17½" (6 x 44.5cm) One 2½" x 18½" (6 x 47cm) One 7" x 10" (17.8 x 25.4cm) cutout using the peace sign section template
Color 4	1 FQ	One 2½" x 19½" (6 x 49.5cm) One 15" x 15" (38.1 x 38.1cm)
Color 5	1 FQ	One 2½" x 17½" (6 x 44.5cm) One 2½" x 18½" (6 x 47cm)
Background	⅔ yd. (61cm)	One 21" x 21" (53.3 x 53.3cm) Two 2½" x 1½" (6 x 4cm) Two 2½" x 2½" (6 x 6cm) Three 2½" x 3½" (6 x 8.9cm) One 2½" x 4½" (6 x 11.4cm)
Backing	1 yd. (90cm)	
Binding	¼ yd. (22.9cm)	Three 2½" (6cm) x WOF sewn end to end

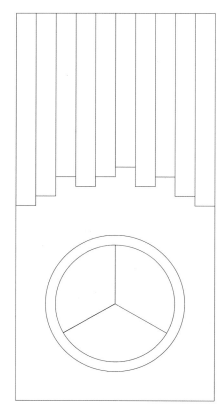

Copy and color in the black-and-white diagram to test different color arrangements before you cut!

Peace Sign Block

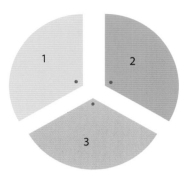

1. To sew the peace sign sections together, you will connect them in a Y-seam. Start by marking ¼" (6mm) away from the center point on each section with a marking pen/pencil. Label the sections 1, 2, and 3.

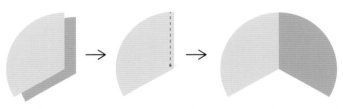

2. With RST, sew Sections 1 and 2 together along one of the straight sides, stopping at the ¼" (6mm) mark from the center, and back stitch. Open the pieces up and press the seam to one side.

3. With right sides up, lay Section 3 in the missing section of the circle with Sections 1 and 2. Align one edge of Section 3 with the edge next to it and pin RST. Sew along the edge, stopping ¼" (6mm) away from the center mark, and back stitch. Do the same with the last edge of the section. Press the seams so that they all face the same direction (in a circular pinwheel).

Inset Circles

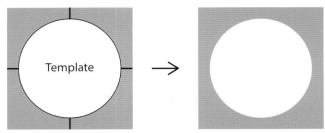

1. Take the 15" x 15" (38.1x 38.1cm) Color 4 piece and cut the peace sign inner border template (11½" [29.2cm] diameter) out of the center of the fabric. To find the center, fold the square in half, then in half again, pressing the creases.

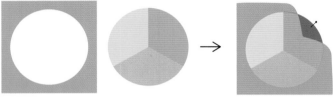

2. Place the Color 4 frame piece on top of the peace sign, both with right sides up. Going around the circle of the peace sign, flip the curved edge of the frame piece so that right sides are together and the raw edges align. Pin all along the circle. Sew and press toward the center of the circle.

3. Place the peace sign border outer circle template (14" [35.6cm] diameter) over your block, centering the template on the fabric, and cut around the template.

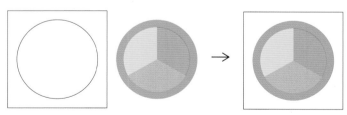

4. Follow Step 1 with the 21"x 21" (53.3 x 53.3cm) background piece and the peace sign background circle template (13½" [34.3cm] diameter). Then follow Step 2 to place the peace sign into the background circle fabric. Press toward the center of the circle. Trim the block to 20½" x 20½" (52.1 x 52.1cm).

Strip Block

1. Take the 19½" (49.5cm) Color 1 and Color 4 strips and sew a 1½" x 2½" (4 x 6cm) background piece to one end of each. Press toward the color.

2. Take the 18½" (47cm) Color 3 and Color 5 strips and sew a 2½" x 2½" (6 x 6cm) background piece to one end of each. Press toward the color.

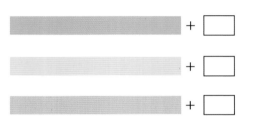

3. Take the 17½" (44.5cm) Color 1, Color 3, and Color 5 strips and sew a 3½" x 2½" (8.9 x 6cm) background piece to one end of each. Press toward the color.

4. Take the 16½" (41.9cm) Color 2 strip and sew a 3½" x 2½" (8.9 x 6cm) background piece to one end of each. Press toward the color.

20.5" x 2.5"

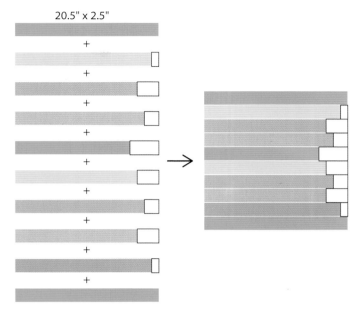

5. Arrange the strip pieces, including the two 20½" x 2½" (52.1 x 6cm) strips, as shown in the illustration and sew them together. Press all seams to one side.

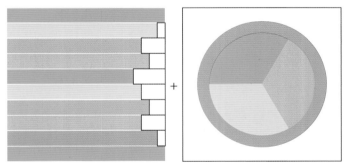

6. Quilt and bind. Note: If you are going to add any pockets or tabs for hanging your mini, do so before finishing with binding.

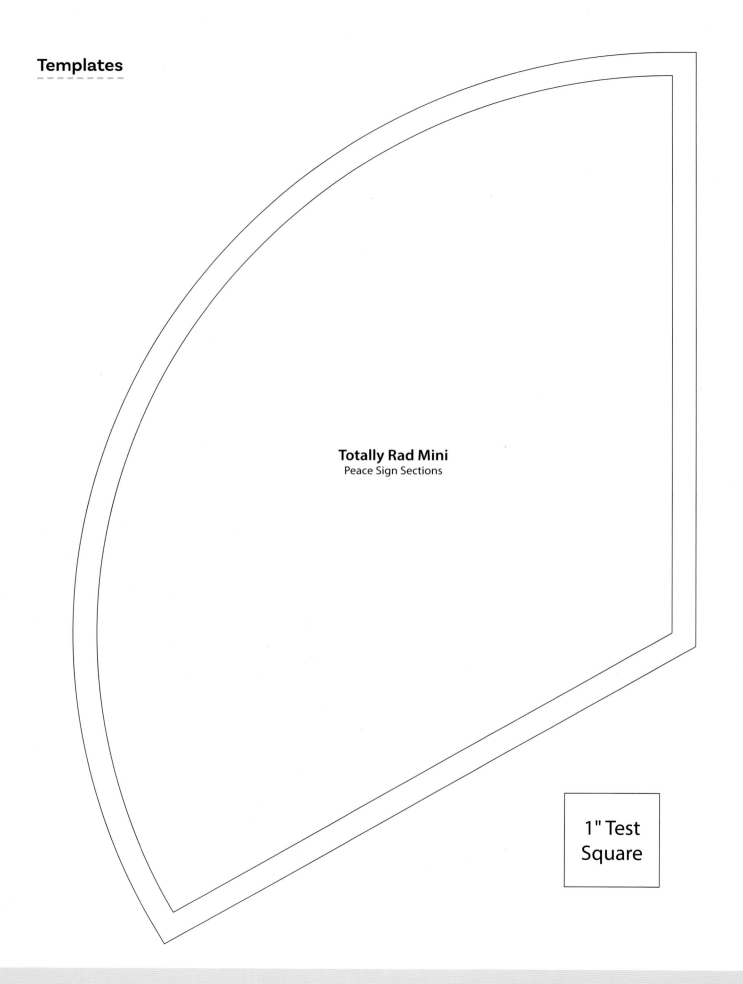

Totally Rad Mini
Peace Sign Sections

1" Test
Square

Totally Rad Mini
Peace Sign Border Inner Circle Template
11.5" diameter circle

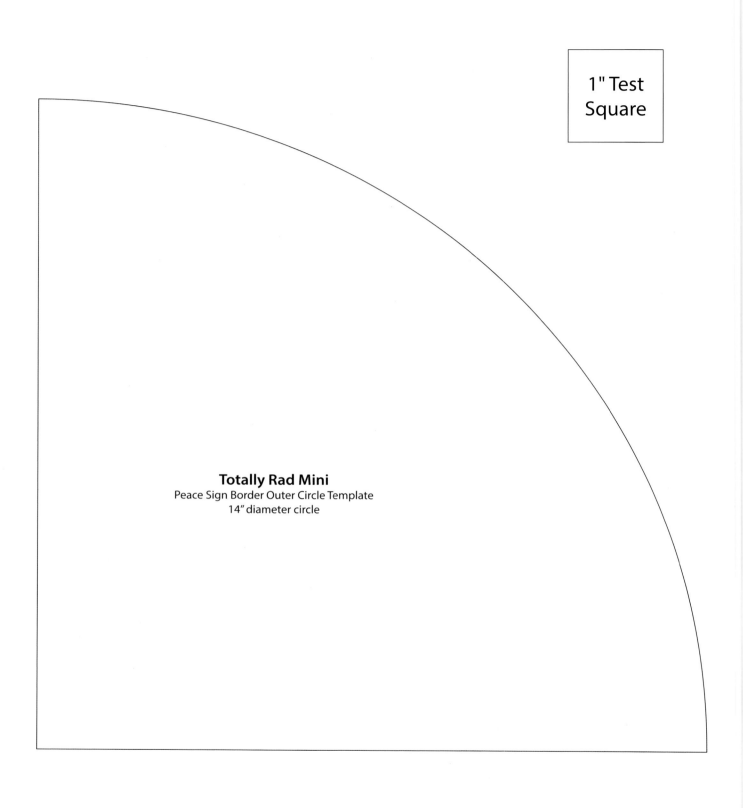

1" Test
Square

Totally Rad Mini
Peace Sign Border Outer Circle Template
14" diameter circle

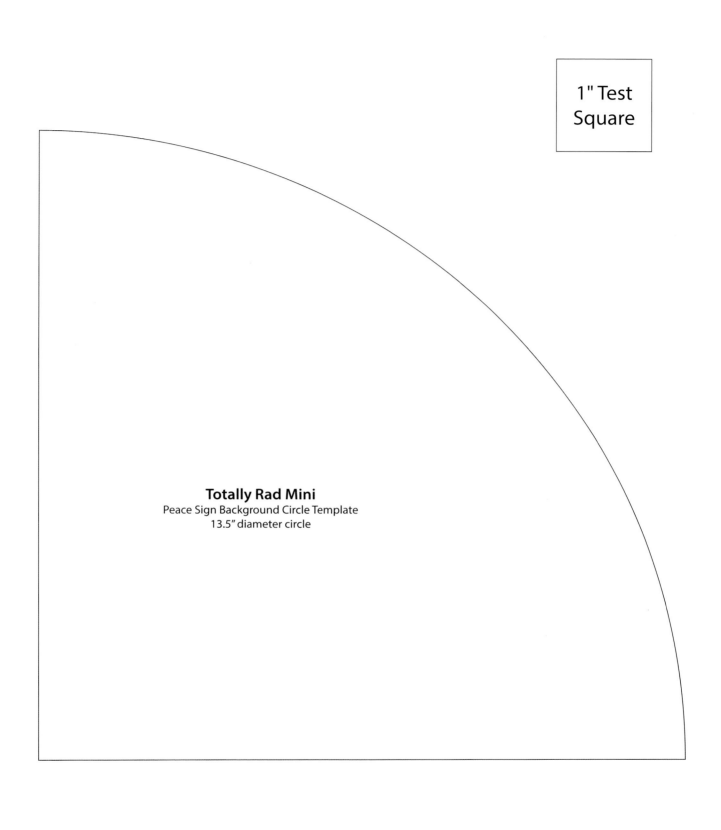

1" Test Square

Totally Rad Mini
Peace Sign Background Circle Template
13.5" diameter circle

Tidal Bloom and Couching Tutorial

By Erin Grogan of Love Sew Modern

The Tidal Bloom mini quilt pattern is named for the jellyfish. A group of jellyfish is referred to as a "smack" or a "bloom." The pulsating movements of a bloom of jellyfish through the ocean can stir up as much vigor as any tide. In this project, the bodies of the jellyfish are pieced with half-circles. It uses big stitch quilting to represent their tentacles and chunky yarn couching to represent their oral arms (see the couching tutorial on page 92). Play with varying thread weights and colors to create the depth and movement of the tentacles and oral arms.

MATERIALS NEEDED

- See Fabric Requirements at right
- Rotary cutter
- Cutting mat
- Fabric scissors
- Fabric marking pen
- Needle
- Thread
- Pins
- Quilting ruler
- Batting
- Couching materials, see page 92

Before You Start

- The finished size of the quilt is 25" x 30½" (63.5 x 77.5cm).
- The WOF is assumed to be 42" (106.7cm).
- The binding width is assumed to be 2¼" (5.7cm).
- The seam allowance is ¼" (6mm) unless otherwise noted.
- Print templates at 100 percent, not "fit to page." Measure the 1" (2.5cm) reference square on your printout to ensure that everything is the correct size.

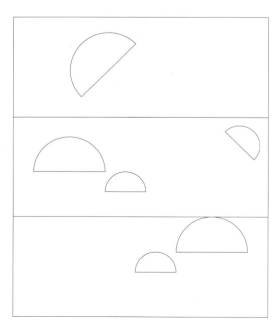

Copy and color in the black-and-white diagram to test different color arrangements before you cut!

FABRIC REQUIREMENTS

Color 1	1 FQ
Color 2	½ yd. (45.7cm)
Color 3	½ yd. (45.7)
Color 4	½ yd. (45.7cm)

CUTTING INSTRUCTIONS

Color 1	Three each of Templates B and D
Color 2	One each of Templates A and C One 2½" x 7½" (6 x 19.1cm) One 3" x 10½" (7.6 x 26.7cm) One 4" x 4½" (10 x 11.4cm) One 5" x 11½" (12.7 x 29.2cm) One 10½" x 11½" (26.7 x 29.2cm)
Color 3	Two Template A One Template C One 2" (5cm) square One 2½" x 6" (6 x 15.2cm) One 2½" x 7½" (6 x 19.1cm) One 2½" x 13½" (6 x 34.3cm) One 3" x 13½" (7.6 x 34.3cm) One 3½" (8.9cm) square One 4" x 4½" (10 x 11.4cm) One 4½" x 6½" (11.4 x 16.5cm) One 8" x 10½" (20.3 x 26.7cm)
Color 4	One Template C One 6" (15.2cm) square One 3¼" x 7¾" (8.3 x 19.7cm) One 3½" (8.9cm) square One 4½" x 10½" (11.4 x 26.7cm) One 10½" x 13¾" (26.7 x 34.9cm) One 3½" (8.9cm) square

Small Half-Circle Blocks

Follow Step 1 below to assemble three small half-circle blocks. Make two blocks using a Color 3 Template A and a Color 1 Template B. Make one block using a Color 2 Template A and a Color 1 Template B.

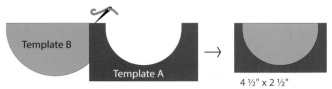

1. Place Template A RST with the Template B piece as shown in the diagram. Sew the pieces together, gently nesting the curve of Template A along the curve of Template B. Snip into the seam roughly every inch without cutting into the stitching. Press toward Template A. Square the block to 4½" x 2½" (11.4 x 6cm).

Large Half-Circle Blocks

Follow Step 1 below to assemble three large half-circle blocks. Make one block using a Color 4 Template C and a Color 1 Template D. Make one block using a Color 3 Template C and a Color 1 Template D. Make one block using a Color 2 Template C and a Color 1 Template D.

1. Place Template C RST with Template D as shown in the diagram. Sew the pieces together, gently nesting the curve of Template C along the curve of Template D. Snip into the seam roughly every inch without cutting into the stitching. Press toward Template C. Square the block to 7½" x 4" (19.1 x 10cm).

The jellyfish tentacles and oral arms are added with couching and big stitch quilting to create gorgeous texture and motion.

Section 1 Assembly

1. Cut a 6" (15.2cm) Color 4 square in half diagonally. Sew one half to the top and one half to the bottom of the Color 4 large half-circle block. Be sure to center the pieces before sewing. Press toward the Color 4 pieces. Trim the excess corners.

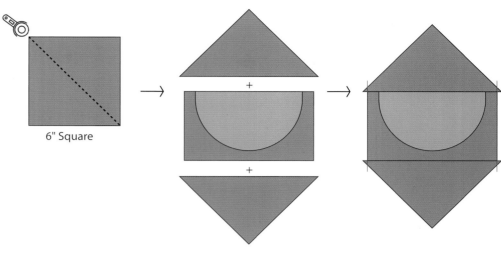

6" Square

2. Cut a 3½" (8.9cm) Color 4 square in half diagonally. Sew one half onto each side of the large half-circle block as shown in the diagram. Press toward the Color 4 pieces. Square the block to 7¾" (19.7cm) square.

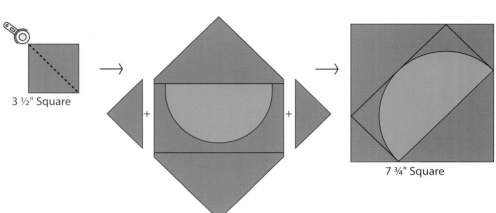

3 ½" Square

7 ¾" Square

3. Sew a 7¾" x 3¼" (19.7 x 8.3cm) Color 4 strip to the bottom of the block. Sew a 4½" x 10½" (11.4 x 26.7cm) Color 4 strip to the left of the unit. Sew a 13¾" x 10½" (34.9 x 26.7cm) Color 4 piece to the right of the unit. Press toward the Color 4 pieces. This completes Section 1, finishing at 25" x 10½" (63.5 x 26.7cm).

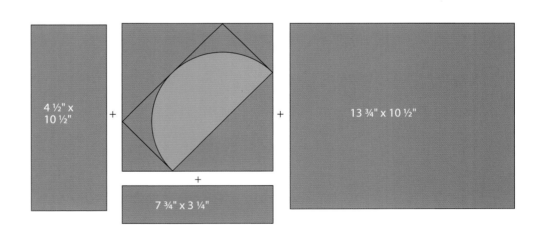

4 ½" x 10 ½"

13 ¾" x 10 ½"

7 ¾" x 3 ¼"

Section 2 Assembly

1. Cut a 3½" (8.9cm) Color 3 square in half diagonally. Sew one half to the top and one half to the bottom of the Color 3 small half-circle block. Press toward the Color 3 pieces.

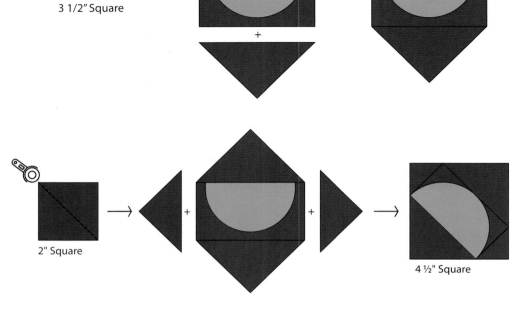

3 1/2" Square

2. Cut a 2" (5cm) Color 3 square in half diagonally. Sew one half onto either side of the unit as shown in the diagram. Press toward the Color 3 pieces. Square the block to 4½" (11.4cm) square.

2" Square

4 ½" Square

3. Sew a 4½" x 6½" (11.4 x 16.5cm) Color 3 piece to the bottom of the block. Sew a 8" x 10½" (20.3 x 26.7cm) Color 3 piece to the left of the unit as shown in the diagram. Press toward the Color 3 pieces. This completes Section 2A.

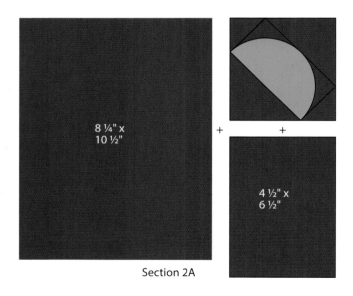

8 ¼" x 10 ½"

4 ½" x 6 ½"

Section 2A

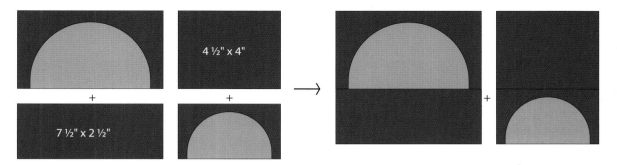

4. Sew a 7½" x 2½" (19.1 x 6cm) Color 3 strip to the bottom of a Color 3 large half-circle block. Sew a 4½" x 4" (11.4 x 10cm) Color 3 piece to the top of a Color 3 small half-circle block. Press toward the Color 3 pieces. Sew the two units together as shown in the diagram.

5. Sew a 6" x 2½" (15.2 x 6cm) Color 3 strip to the left of the unit as shown in the diagram. Sew a 13½" x 3" (34.3 x 7.6cm) Color 3 strip to the bottom of the unit. Sew a 13½" x 2½" (34.3 x 6cm) Color 3 strip to the top of the unit. Press toward the Color 3 strips. This completes Section 2B.

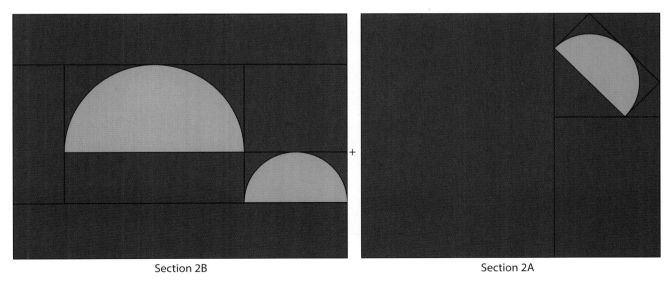

Section 2B   Section 2A

6. Sew Section 2A to the right side of Section 2B. Press toward Section 2A. This completes Section 2, finishing at 25" x 10½" (63.5 x 26.7cm).

Section 3 Assembly

1. Sew a 4½" x 4" (11.4 x 10cm) Color 2 piece to the top of a Color 2 small half-circle block. Sew a 7½" x 2½" (19.1 x 6cm) Color 2 piece to the bottom of a Color 2 large half-circle block. Press toward the Color 2 pieces. Sew the two units together as shown in the diagram.

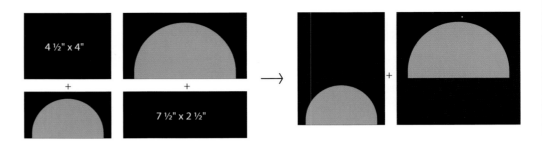

2. Sew a 11½" x 5" (29.2x 12.7cm) Color 2 piece to the bottom of the unit. Sew a 3" x 10½" (7.6 x 26.7cm) Color 2 strip to the right of the unit. Sew a 12½" x 10½" (31.8 x 26.7cm) Color 2 piece to the left of the unit. Press toward the Color 2 pieces. This completes Section 3, finishing at 25" x 10½" (63.5 x 26.7cm).

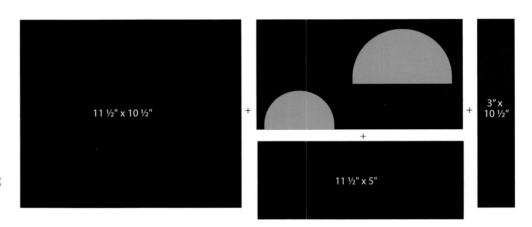

Quilt Top Assembly

1. Sew the three sections together as shown in the diagram.

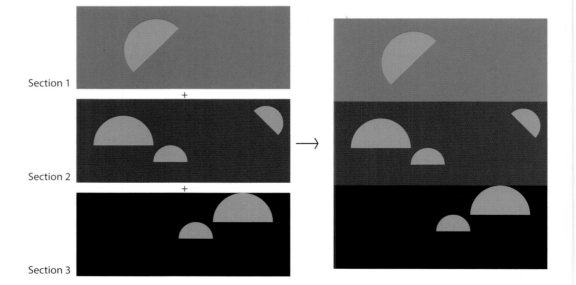

This quilt is great to use on beach holidays, but works equally well as decoration in your house, vacation home, or camper.

Templates

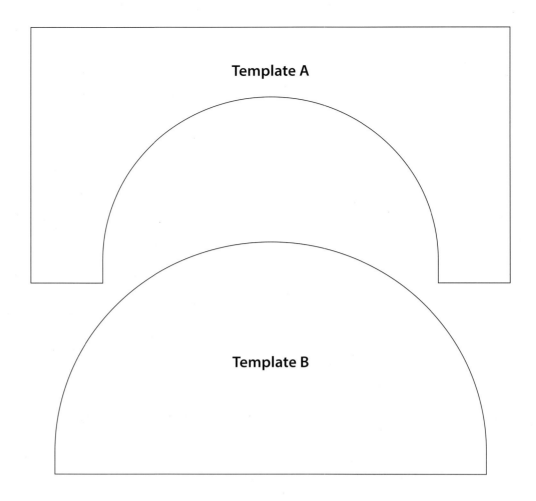

Template A

Template B

1" Test Square

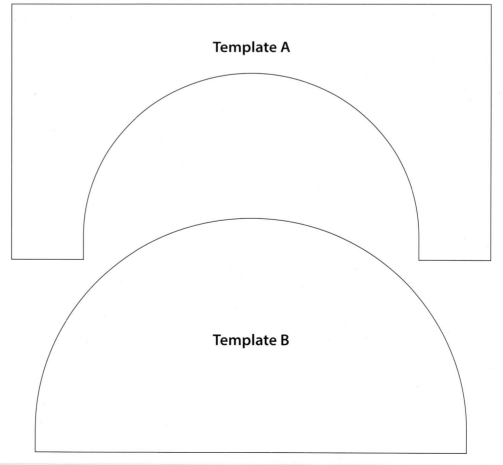

Template A

Template B

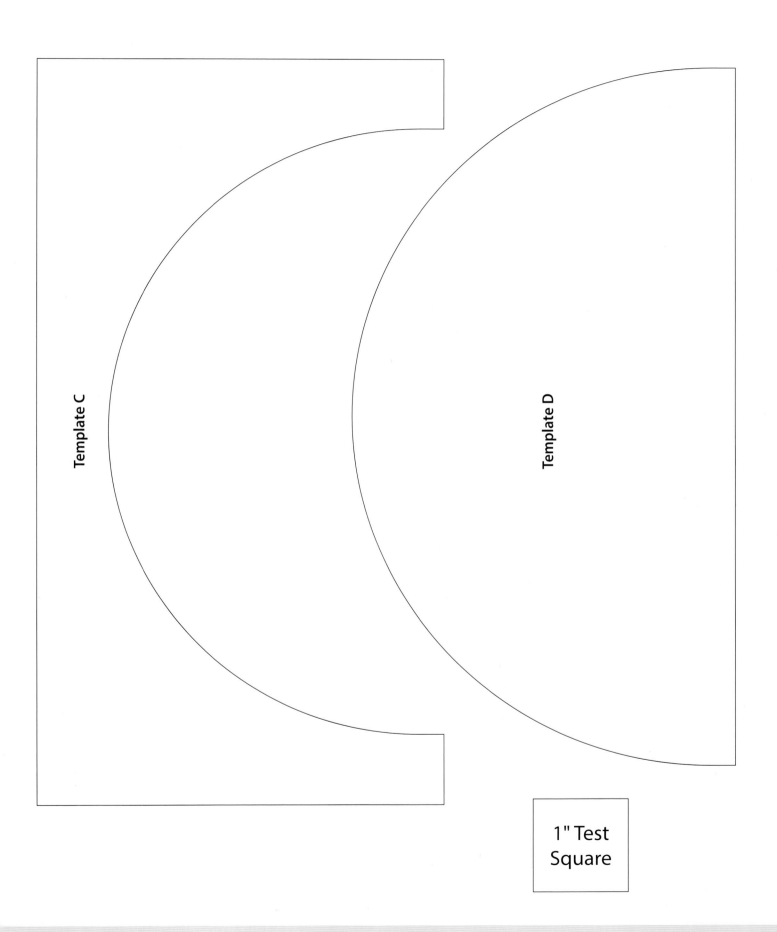

Template C

Template D

1" Test Square

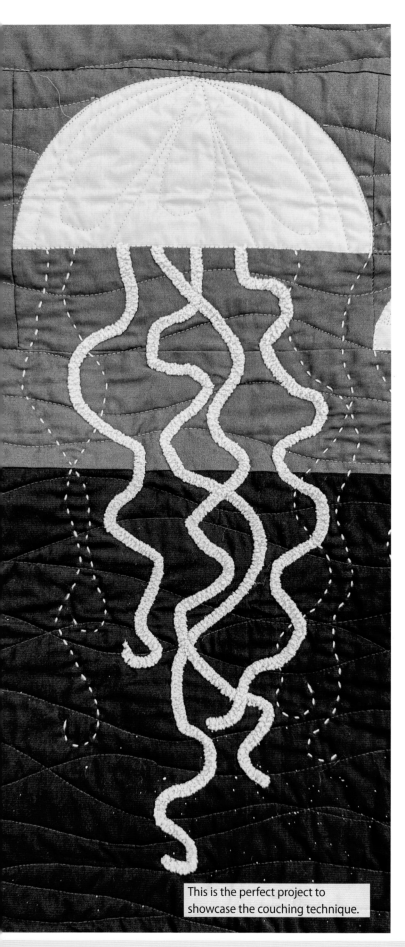

This is the perfect project to showcase the couching technique.

Couching Tutorial

Couching is a great and easy technique for adding texture to your sewing projects. There are special sewing-machine feet made for couching. They're typically referred to as either a cording foot or a braiding foot. This foot has a beveled hole for cords and yarns that provides smooth and even couching. However, if you're new to this technique and don't want to invest in a new foot for your machine, any decorative stitch foot you have will work. You will be using the zigzag stitch, which is why you need a foot that works with decorative stitching. Couching feels a lot like blending the skills of raw-edge appliqué and free-motion quilting.

You can play with different weights of yarn or cords with the couching technique. If your machine offers a variety of decorative stitches, you can also experiment with different stitches. Most importantly, have fun while experimenting with couching.

MATERIALS NEEDED

- Yarn or cord, up to ½" (1.5cm) in width
- 50wt yarn/cording-coordinated thread
- 50wt backing-coordinated thread
- Cording foot or decorative-stitch foot

1. On a piece of scrap fabric, test the width and length settings of your stitch. You want your zigzag stitch to fully cover the width of what you're couching.

2. Leaving a 1"–2" (2.5–5cm) tail, place the yarn or cord where you'd like to begin. Stitch two or three times followed by two or three back stitches.

3. With your nondominant hand, hold the working end of your yarn straight toward your chest. It helps to place the yarn ball in a bowl to control it as it unwinds.

4. Moving slowly, zigzag stitch over the yarn. With your dominant hand, move the quilt under the needle, creating the design. It's important to take your time and move slowly.

5. When you arrive at your stopping point, back stitch multiple times to secure the end of your yarn.

6. With scissors, snip off the excess yarn and thread at your starting and stopping points, being careful not to cut into your back stitches.

COUCHING TIPS

- The fuzzier the yarn, the more difficult it will be to control.
- Move slowly.
- Keep your needle down when lifting your foot or pivoting.
- Don't pull your working yarn up while sewing it down because you will also pull your bobbin threads to the top.
- If you couch directly onto only the quilt top, it will gather and pull unevenly. To prevent this, stabilize your quilt top by basting the batting to the back. You can apply the couching technique through all three layers of your quilt as well, if desired.

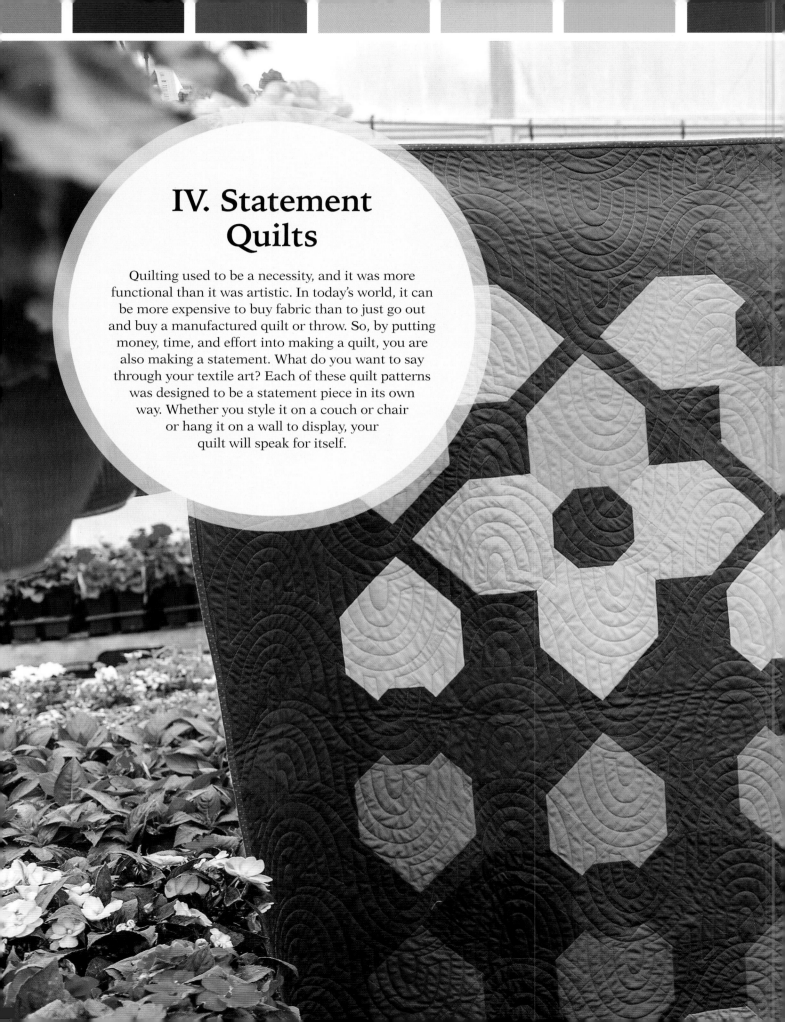

IV. Statement Quilts

Quilting used to be a necessity, and it was more functional than it was artistic. In today's world, it can be more expensive to buy fabric than to just go out and buy a manufactured quilt or throw. So, by putting money, time, and effort into making a quilt, you are also making a statement. What do you want to say through your textile art? Each of these quilt patterns was designed to be a statement piece in its own way. Whether you style it on a couch or chair or hang it on a wall to display, your quilt will speak for itself.

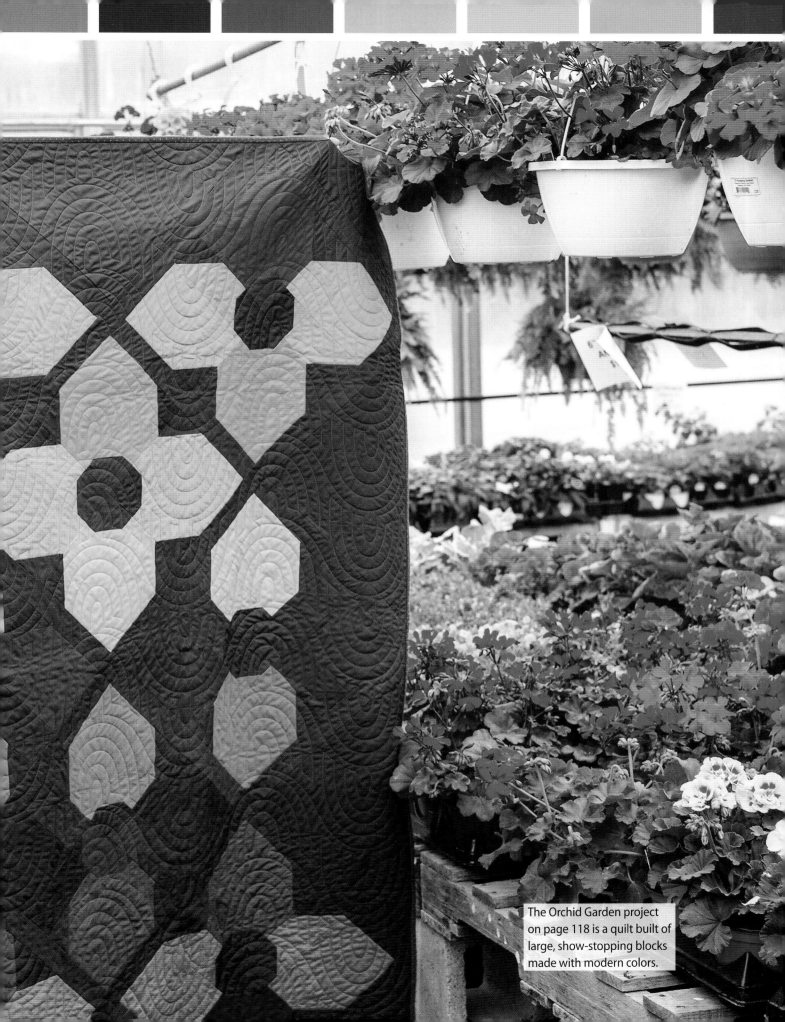

The Orchid Garden project on page 118 is a quilt built of large, show-stopping blocks made with modern colors.

Color Code

By Kiley Ferons of Kiley's Quilting Room

Talk about a color explosion! I love that this quilt uses only color and has no background. This quilt makes for a great gift for artists in your life, children, teachers—pretty much anyone crafty. Use all the colors of the rainbow or your own favorite color palette.

MATERIALS NEEDED

- See Fabric Requirements below
- Rotary cutter
- Cutting mat
- Fabric scissors
- Fabric marking pen
- Needle
- Thread
- Pins
- Quilting ruler
- Batting

Before You Start

- Read through all the instructions first.
- The finished size of the quilt is 54" x 66" (137.2 x 167.6cm).
- The WOF is assumed to be 42" (106.7cm).
- The seam allowance is ¼" (6mm) unless otherwise noted.
- Print the templates at 100 percent, not "fit to page." Measure the 1" (2.5cm) reference square on your printout to ensure that everything is the correct size.
- When posting online or searching for ideas for your quilt, use or search the hashtag #ColorCodeQuilt.

Copy and color in the black-and-white diagram to test different color arrangements before you cut!

FABRIC REQUIREMENTS

	Throw 54" x 66" (137.2 x 167.6cm)
One tan color for pencil wood	2¼ yds. (2.1m)
Thirty-six assorted colors for pencils/backgrounds	1 F8 each
Backing	3½ yds. (3.2m)
Binding	½ yd. (45.7cm)

CUTTING INSTRUCTIONS

Tan (pencil wood)	Thirty-six assorted colors (for each color)
Six 9½" (24.1cm) x WOF, Subcut: Thirty-six 9½" x 7" (24.1 x 17.8cm)	One 2" x 22" (5 x 55.9cm), Subcut: Six 2" x 2" (5 x 5cm) One 2" x 9½" (5 x 24.1cm)
Six 3½" (8.9cm) x WOF, Subcut: One hundred eight 3½" x 2" (8.9 x 5cm)	One 5½" x 22" (14 x 55.9cm), Subcut: One [if using solids] or Two [if using prints or single-sided fabric] 5½" x 9½" (14 x 24.1cm) One 3" x 4" (7.6 x 10cm)

Assembling the Blocks

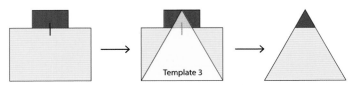

1. Find the center of the 9½" x 7" (24.1 x 17.8cm) tan pieces and the 3" x 4" (7.6 x 10cm) pieces of each color. With RST, align the center marks of one tan piece and one color piece, then sew them together. Press toward the color fabric. Then, use Template 3 to cut out a triangle from this block, as shown in the diagram. Repeat with the remaining tan and color pieces, giving you a total of thirty-six blocks, each a different color.

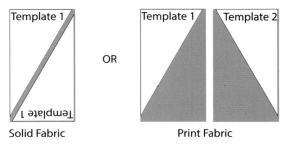

2. If you are using solids for your colors, the fabric is double-sided, so you can cut two Template 1s from one 5½" x 9½" (14 x 24.1cm) piece, as shown in the diagram. If your fabric is printed and has a definite right and wrong side, you'll need two 5½" x 9½" (14 x 24.1cm) pieces to cut a Template 1 and a Template 2.

3. Either on paper or by laying out your blocks, decide where you want to place your colors. The Template 1 and 2 pieces that match a block's color will attach to the block below it (if it is the top row, you will use the bottom row's color Template 1 and 2 pieces). See the color assembly guide on page 99 for reference.

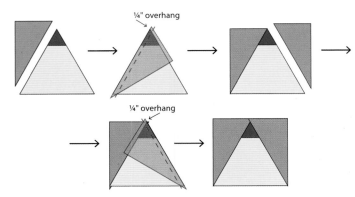

4. Place the template pieces so that the diagonal edges align with the diagonal edges of the triangle. Align the pieces, RST, with a ¼" (6mm) overhang at the top. Sew a *scant* ¼" (6mm) seam and press away from the tan triangle. Do the same to the other side with the other template piece of the same color. Trim the block to 9½"x 8½" (24.1 x 21.6cm), making sure to leave ¼" (6mm) of space above the point of the pencil.

5. Mark a diagonal line on the backs of all 2" x 2" (5 x 5cm) squares from each color. With RST, align one of those squares to one end of a 3½" x 2" (8.9 x 5cm) tan piece, as shown in the diagram. Sew on the diagonal, press, and trim the excess off. Do the same to the other side of the tan piece, as shown in the diagram. Make three of these flying geese blocks for each color. Trim each one to 3½" x 2" (8.9 x 5cm).

6. Sew the three flying geese blocks of each color together in a row, as shown in the diagram. Press the seams open.

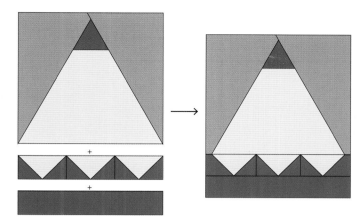

8. Assemble the blocks into rows. Make sure that the color placement works and that each block matches with the block above or below it. See the color assembly guide below for assistance.

9. Sew the rows together first, then press the seams in each row in the opposite direction from the row before it; this way, your blocks seams will nest.

10. Quilt and bind as desired.

7. Sew the matching 2" x 9½" (5 x 24.1cm) strips to the bottom of the flying geese row, matching the colors. Sew the matching pencil point block to the top. Press the seams to one side. Each finished block should measure 9½" x 11½" (24.1 x 29.2cm). You should have thirty-six blocks.

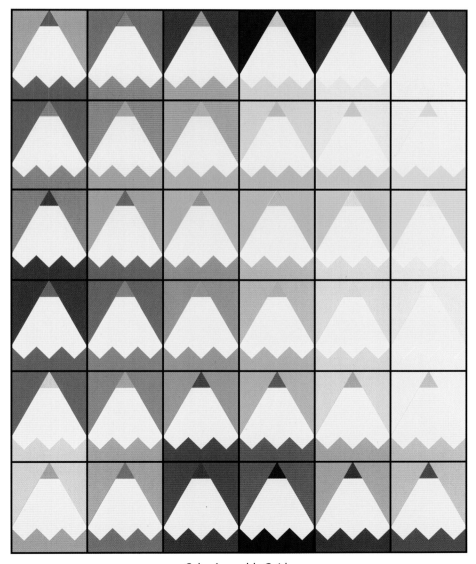

Color Assembly Guide

Templates

Template 1

1" Test Square

Template 3

Tape to other side of Template 3

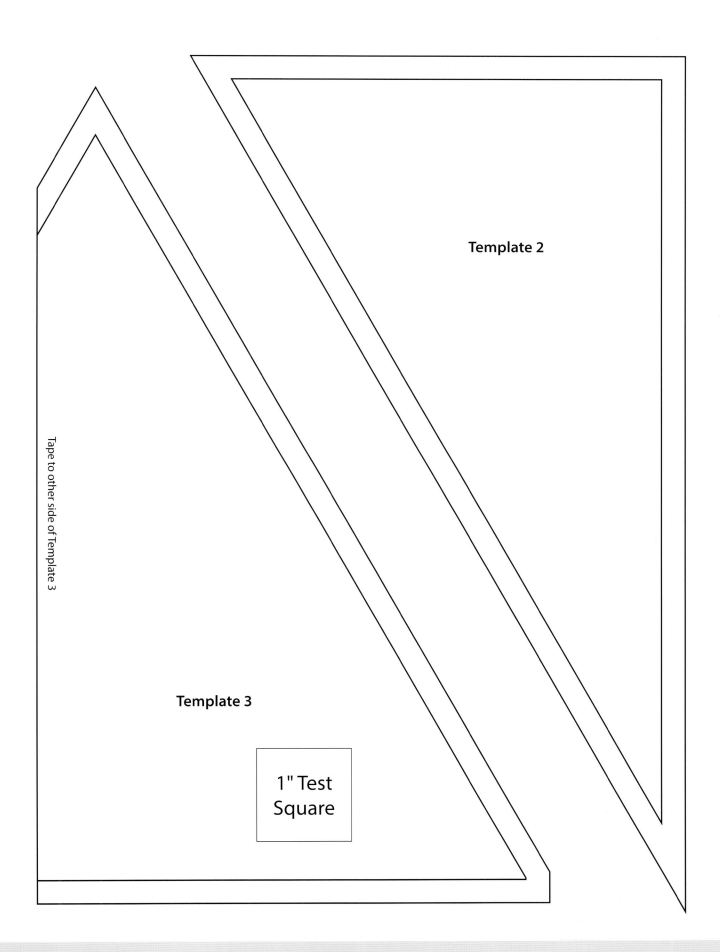

Template 2

Tape to other side of Template 3

Template 3

1" Test
Square

Baseline

By Kiley Ferons of Kiley's Quilting Room

There's something about an ombre effect that just makes my heart sing! This pattern is sure to turn heads whether made with stunning ombre colors or two-tone contrast! It's a simple design that really stands out.

MATERIALS NEEDED

- See Fabric Requirements below
- Rotary cutter
- Cutting mat
- Fabric scissors
- Fabric marking pen
- Needle
- Thread
- Pins
- Quilting ruler
- Batting

Before You Start

- The seam allowance is ¼" (6mm) unless otherwise noted.
- Press all seams to the color side.
- Share your quilt on Instagram with the hashtag #BaselineQuilt.

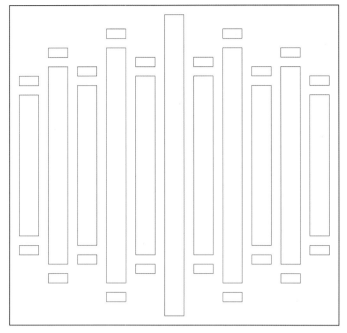

Copy and color in the black-and-white diagram to test different color arrangements before you cut!

FABRIC REQUIREMENTS

	Baby 40" x 40" (101.6 x 101.6cm)	Throw 68" x 68" (172.7 x 172.7cm)
Background	1¼ yds. (1.1m)	2½ yds. (2.3m)
Ombre Version: Six Colors	¼ yd. (22.9cm) of each color	½ yd. (45.7cm) of each color
Two-Tone Version: One Color	⅔ yd. (61cm)	2 yds. (1.8m)
Binding	⅓ yd. (30.5cm)	½ yd. (45.7cm)
Backing	3 yds. (2.7m)	4⅔ yds. (4.3m)

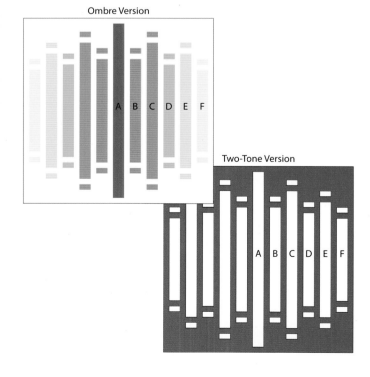

Ombre Version

Two-Tone Version

CUTTING INSTRUCTIONS

	Baby Ombre	Baby Two-Tone	Throw Ombre	Throw Two-Tone
Background	Fourteen 2" (5 cm) x WOF, Subcut: Two 2" x 40½" (5 x 102.9cm) Twelve 2" x 37½" (5 x 95.3cm) One 2½" (6cm) x WOF, Subcut: Twenty 2½" x 1½" (6 x 4cm), Label Z Three 2½" (6cm) x WOF Sew end to end, Subcut: Four 2½" x 5" (6 x 12.7cm), Label L Four 2½" x 2" (6 x 5cm), Label M Four 2½" x 6" (6 x 15.2cm), Label N Four 2½" x 4½" (6 x 11.4cm), Label O Four 2½" x 8" (6 x 20.3cm), Label P		Twenty-four 2½" (6cm) x WOF Sew end to end, Subcut: Two 2½" x 68½" (6 x 174cm) Twelve 2½" x 64½" (6 x 163.8cm) Twenty 2½" x 4½" (6 x 11.4cm), Label Z Five 4½" (11.4cm) x WOF Sew end to end, Subcut: Four 4½" x 9½" (11.4 x 24.1cm), Label L Four 4½" x 3½" (11.4 x 8.9cm), Label M Four 4½" x 11½" (11.4 x 29.2cm), Label N Four 4½" x 7½" (11.4 x 19.1cm), Label O Four 4½" x 13½" (11.4 x 34.3cm), Label P	
Color A	One 2½" (6cm) x WOF, Subcut: One 2½" x 37½" (6 x 95.3cm)		Two 4½" (11.4cm) x WOF Sew end to end, Subcut: One 4½" x 64½" (11.4 x 163.8cm)	
Color B	Two 2½" (6cm) x WOF, Subcut: Two 2½" x 24½" (6 x 62.2cm) Four 2½" x 1½" (6 x 4cm) Label BX		Three 4½" (11.4cm) x WOF , Subcut: Two 4½" x 38½" (11.4 x 97.8cm) Four 4½" x 2½" (11.4 x 6cm) Label BX	
Color C	Two 2½" (6cm) x WOF, Subcut: Two 2½" x 30½" (6 x 77.5cm) Four 2½" x 1½" (6 x 4cm) Label CX	Eight 2½" (6cm) x WOF Sew end to end, Subcut: One 2½" x 37½" (6 x 95.3cm), Label A Two 2½" x 24½" (6 x 62.2cm), Label B Two 2½" x 30½" (6 x 77.5cm), Label C Two 2½" x 22½" (6 x 57.2cm), Label D Two 2½" x 25½" (6 x 64.8cm), Label E Two 2½" x 18½" (6 x 47cm), Label F Twenty 2½" x 1½" (6 x 4cm), Label X	Three 4½" (11.4cm) x WOF Sew end to end, Subcut: Two 4½" x 50½" (11.4 x 128.3cm) Four 4½" x 2½" (11.4 x 6cm) Label CX	Thirteen 4½" (11.4cm) x WOF Sew end to end, Subcut: One 4½" x 64½" (11.4 x 163.8cm), Label A Two 4½" x 38½" (11.4 x 97.8cm), Label B Two 4½" x 50½" (11.4 x 128.3cm), Label C Two 4½" x 34½" (11.4 x 87.6cm), Label D Two 4½" x 42½" (11.4 x 108cm), Label E Two 4½" x 30½" (11.4 x 77.5cm), Label F Twenty 4½" x 2½" (11.4 x 6cm), Label X
Color D	Two 2½" (6cm) x WOF, Subcut: Two 2½" x 22½" (6 x 57.2cm) Four 2½" x 1½" (6 x 4cm) Label DX		Two 4½" (11.4cm) x WOF, Subcut: Two 4½" x 34½" (11.4 x 87.6cm) Four 4½" x 2½" (11.4 x 6cm) Label DX	
Color E	Two 2½" (6cm) x WOF Subcut: Two 2½" x 25½" (6 x 64.8cm) Four 2½" x 1½" (6 x 4cm) Label EX		Three 4½" (11.4cm) x WOF , Subcut: Two 4½" x 42½" (11.4 x 108cm) Four 4½" x 2½" (11.4 x 6cm) Label EX	
Color F	Two 2½" (6cm) x WOF, Subcut: Two 2½" x 18½" (6 x 47cm) Four 2½" x 1½" (6 x 4cm) Label FX		Two 4½" (11.4cm) x WOF, Subcut: Two 4½" x 30½" (11.4 x 77.5cm) Four 4½" x 2½" (11.4 x 6cm) Label FX	

Assembling Rows

First, assemble the rows. You will have two of each row, except for Row A, of which you will have only one. All rows should measure 37½" (95.3cm) for baby size or 64½" (163.8cm) for the throw. Press all seams to the darker fabric. **Note:** If you are making the two-toned version, all rows will be the same color.

A

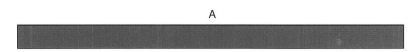

1. Row A: Label this row and set it aside. There is only one Row A.

2. Row B: Sew together in a row with RST the following pieces in this order: Background L, Color BX, Background Z, Color B, Background Z, Color BX, and Background L. Make two of these.

3. Row C: Sew together in a row with RST the following pieces in this order: Background M, Color CX, Background Z, Color C, Background Z, Color CX, and Background M. Make two of these.

4. Row D: Sew together in a row with RST the following pieces in this order: Background N, Color DX, Background Z, Color D, Background Z, Color DX, and Background N. Make two of these.

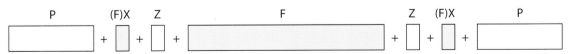

5. Row E: Sew together in a row with RST the following pieces in this order: Background O, Color EX, Background Z, Color E, Background Z, Color EX, and Background O. Make two of these.

6. Row F: Sew together in a row with RST the following pieces in this order: Background P, Color FX, Background Z, Color F, Background Z, Color FX, and Background P. Make two of these.

Assembling the Top

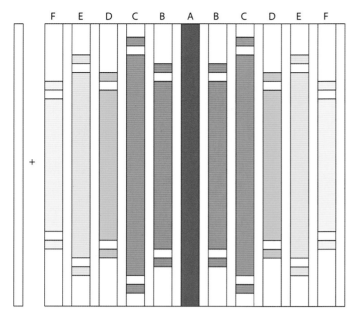

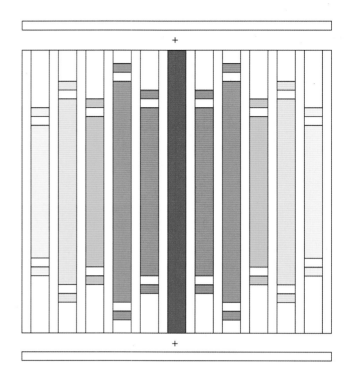

1. Assemble the top, placing a 2" x 37½" (5 x 95.3cm) piece for the baby size or 2½" x 64½" (6 x 163.8cm) piece for the throw in between each row. You will also start and stop with one of these pieces. Press all seams to the same direction.

2. Add a 2" x 40½" (5 x 102.9cm) piece for the baby size or 2½" x 68½" (6 x 174cm) piece for the throw to both the top and bottom of the quilt top. Press the seams toward the background strip.

3. Quilt as desired.

A delicate pattern in complementary colors is the perfect unexpected backing for any modern quilt.

The ombre effect works well with these orange shades, but will be equally striking if made using fabrics from other color families.

Diamond Drizzle

By Kiley Ferons of Kiley's Quilting Room and Elyse Thompson

One of the defining characteristics of a "modern" quilt is having a lot of negative space. Not all modern quilts fall into this category, but it is a great way to make a statement. This quilt has a simple design that is intricate enough to make you stop and wonder. There is plenty of negative space to add detail through your quilting. This quilt is sure to stand out!

MATERIALS NEEDED

- See Fabric Requirements at right
- Rotary cutter
- Cutting mat
- Fabric scissors
- Fabric marking pen
- Needle
- Thread
- Pins
- Quilting ruler
- Batting

Before You Start

- The finished size of the quilt is 61½" x 62½" (156.2 x 158.8cm).
- This pattern uses templates and curved piecing.
- Print the templates at 100 percent, not "fit to page." Measure the 1" (2.5cm) reference square on your printout to ensure that everything is the correct size.
- We recommend printing the templates on card stock for more durability and stability.
- We also recommend printing the labels to help keep your pieces organized.

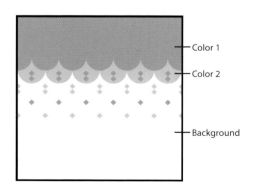

Color 1
Color 2
Background

FABRIC REQUIREMENTS

Background	2¾ yds. (2.5m)
Color 1	2 yds. (1.8m)
Color 2	1 yd. (90cm)
Backing	4 yds. (3.7m)
Binding	½ yd. (45.7cm)

CUTTING INSTRUCTIONS

Background	Cut 2 yds. (1.8m) and follow the cutting diagram on page 110: One 20" x 70" (50.8 x 152.4cm) Six 6" x 11" (15.2 x 27.9cm) Six 7¾" x 7¾" (19.7 x 19.7cm) Twenty-one 4⅜" x 7¾" (11.1 x 19.7cm) Cut two 4⅜" (11.1cm) x WOF, Subcut: Three 4⅜" x 7¾" (11.1 x 19.7cm) Twenty-four 4⅜" x 2" (11.1 x 5cm) Twelve 2" x 2" (5 x 5cm) Cut four 2⅝" (6.7cm) x WOF, Subcut: Twelve 2⅝" x 7¾" (6.7 x 19.7cm) Twelve 2⅝" x 3½" (6.7 x 8.9cm)
Color 1	Cut along the selvage to avoid seams in the big piece. One 16" x 70" (40.6 x 17.8cm) = I Eighteen 2" x 2" (5 x 5cm) = J Six 5½" x 10¾" (14 x 27.3cm) = K Cut one 4½" (11.4cm) x WOF, Subcut: Six 4½" x 6" (11.4 x 15.2cm) = L Cut one 4¼" (10.8cm) x WOF, Subcut: Six 4¼" x 3½" (10.8 x 8.9cm) = M
Color 2	Cut two 2¾" (7cm) x WOF, Subcut: Six 2¾" x 3½" (7 x 8.9cm) = N Six 2¾" x 9½" (7 x 24.1cm) = O Cut two 2" (5cm) x WOF, Subcut: Thirty 2" x 2" (5 x 5cm) = P Cut one 11" (27.9cm) x WOF, Subcut: Six 11" x 6" (27.9 x 15.2cm) = Q

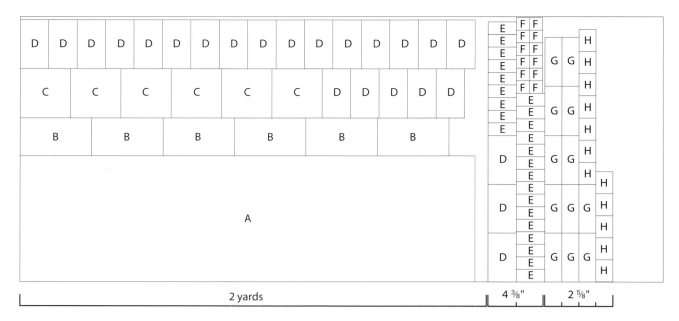

Background Cutting Diagram

Block 1

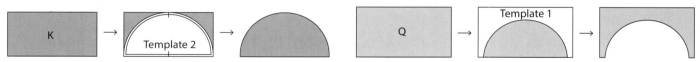

1. Align Template 2 with the K pieces and cut along the curve. Discard the "frame" pieces. Align Template 1 with the Q pieces and cut along the curve. Discard the semicircle pieces. You will have six of each.

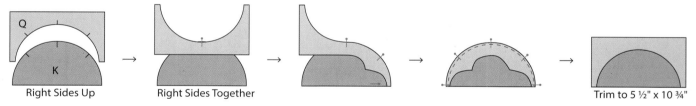

2. Fold each K and Q piece in half, then in half again, and finger-press the folds. Open them back up. Each piece will have three creases. Align a Q piece above a K piece, with right sides up and curves aligned. Then flip the Q piece over so it is RST with the K piece and the tops of each curve and crease are aligned. Pin in place. Continue to force the curve of the Q piece to match the curve of the K piece, matching up and pinning the creases as you go. Pin the ends as shown in the diagram. Sew along the curve. Press the seams to the semicircle and trim the blocks to 5½" x 10¾" (14x 27.3cm). You will have six Block 1s.

Block 2

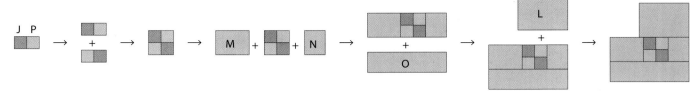

1. Sew one J piece to one P piece. Press the seams to the darker side. Repeat with the eleven remaining J and eleven remaining P pieces to end up with twelve of these sets. Align half of these sets with the darker square on the right and half with the darker square on the left and sew them together to make six four-square blocks. Press the seams. Sew an M piece to the left of each four-square block, and an N piece to the right. Press the seams to one direction. Sew an O piece to the bottom of each block, then press. Sew an L piece to the top of each block, aligning it with the right edge (it will not be the same length as the block as shown in the diagram).

2. Line a ruler up with the corners of the Color 1 squares and the bottom right corner of the block and mark a line. Align the center marks on Template 2 with the diagonal mark you made on the block. Cut out around the template.

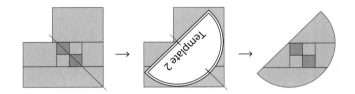

3. Align Template 1 with the B pieces and cut along the curve. Discard the semicircle pieces. You will have six.

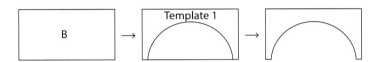

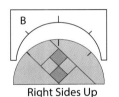

Right Sides Up

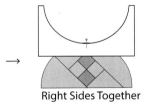

Right Sides Together

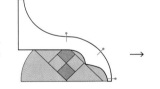

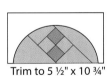

Trim to 5 ½" x 10 ¾"

4. Fold each constructed half-circle and each B piece in half, then in half again, and finger-press the folds. Open them back up. Each piece will have three creases. Align a B piece above the semicircle, with right sides up and curves aligned. Then, flip the B piece over so it is RST with the semicircle and the tops of each curve and crease are aligned. Pin in place. Continue to force the curve of the B piece to match the curve of the semicircle, matching up and pinning the creases as you go. Pin the ends as shown. Sew along the curve. Press the seams to the semicircle and trim the blocks to 5½" x 10¾" (14 x 27.3cm). You will have six Block 2s.

Block 3

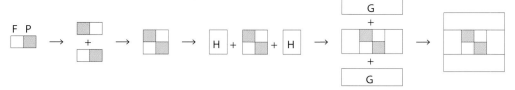

1. Sew one F piece to one P piece. Press the seams to the darker side. Repeat with the eleven remaining J pieces and the eleven remaining P pieces to end up with twelve of these sets. Align half of these sets with the darker square on the right and half with the darker square on the left and sew them together to make six four-square blocks. Press the seams. Sew an H piece to both.sides of each block. Press the seams to one direction. Sew a G piece to the top and bottom of each block. Press the seams. The blocks should measure 7¼" x 7¼" (18.4 x 18.4cm). There will be six Block 3s.

Blocks 4 and 5

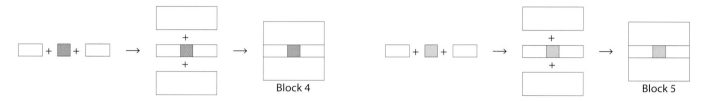

Block 4

Block 5

1. Take six J pieces and six P pieces and sew an E piece to both sides of each. Press the seams to one side. Then sew a D piece to the top and bottom of each. Press the seams to one side. The blocks with a J piece are Block 4s and the blocks with a P piece are Block 5s. There are six of each that should measure 7¼" x 7¼" (18.4 x 18.4cm).

Top Section Assembly

1. Find the center on one of the Block 1s by folding it in half, then cut on the crease. Sew the Block 1s in a row as shown, with the half blocks on the ends as shown. Press the seams to the right.

2. Sew the Block 2s in a row as shown. Press the seams to the left.

3. Sew the rows together, then sew an I piece to the top. Press the seams down.

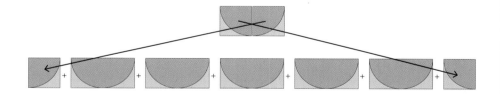

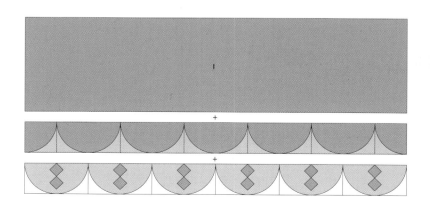

Middle Section Assembly

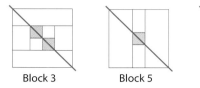

Block 3   Block 5   C

1. Take one Block 3, one Block 5, and one C piece and cut on the diagonal, as shown in the diagram.

2. Sew the rows as shown in the diagram. Do not press them yet.

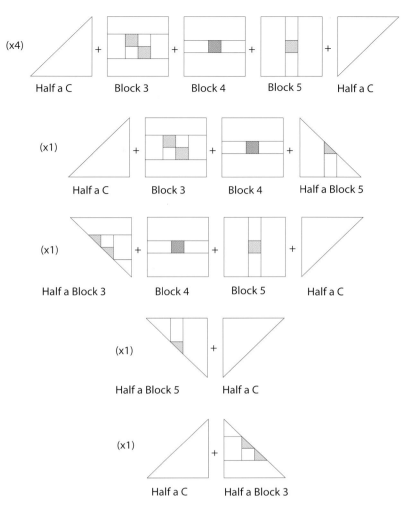

(x4)   Half a C + Block 3 + Block 4 + Block 5 + Half a C

(x1)   Half a C + Block 3 + Block 4 + Half a Block 5

(x1)   Half a Block 3 + Block 4 + Block 5 + Half a C

(x1)   Half a Block 5 + Half a C

(x1)   Half a C + Half a Block 3

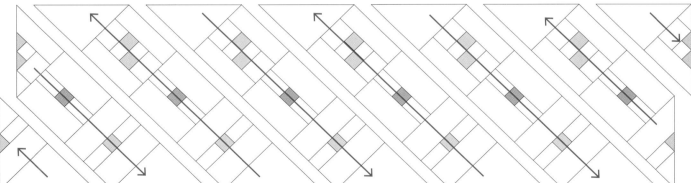

3. Arrange the rows diagonally as shown in the diagram. Starting on one side, press the seams in each row opposite from the row before it.

4. Once all the seams are pressed in each row, sew the rows together. Lay down two rows with RST. Pin the intersection of each block. Because the rows are pressed in opposite directions, the intersecting seams should nest together nicely. When you are done, press all the seams in the same direction.

Quilt Top Assembly

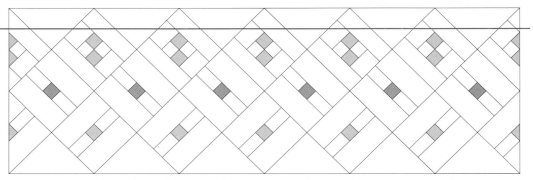

1. Line up a ruler ¼" (6mm) from the top points of the Color 2 squares in the section and mark alignment. Cut along this line.

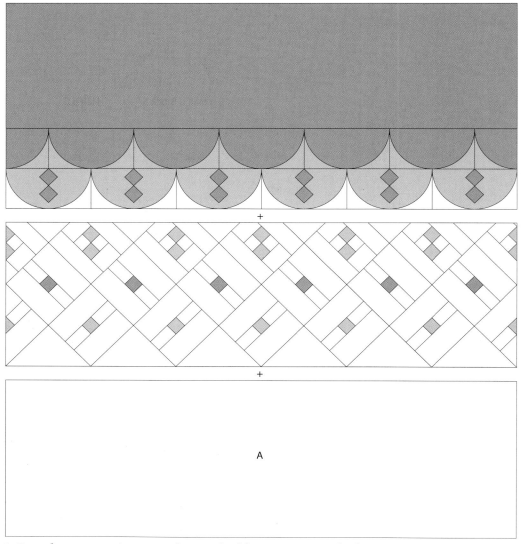

2. Sew the two sections together and add an A piece at the bottom. Press the seams down.

3. Quilt and bind as desired.

This design includes a modern use of negative space that really showcases the quilting and makes this quilt a stunning piece.

Templates

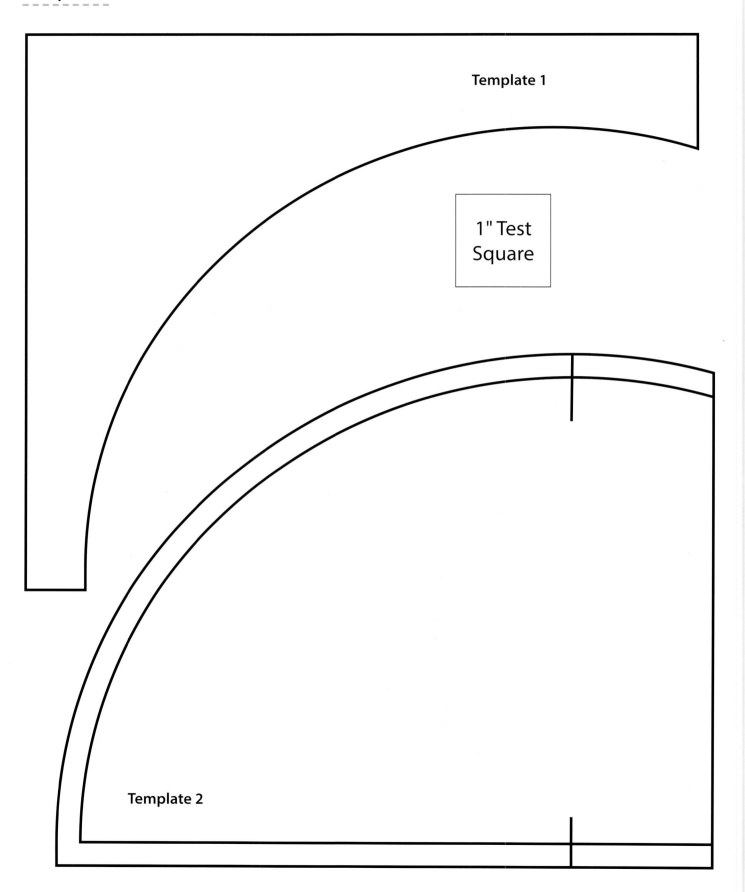

Template 1

1" Test Square

Template 2

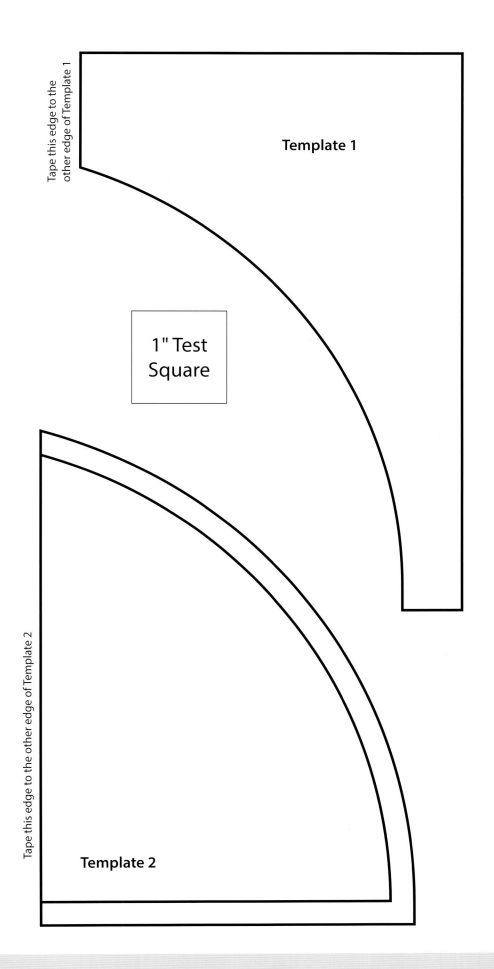

Template 1

Tape this edge to the other edge of Template 1

1" Test
Square

Tape this edge to the other edge of Template 2

Template 2

Orchid Garden

By Meghan Morris of Piece of Quiet Quilts

Both big blocks and tiny blocks have the power to make people stop and stare! These large floral blocks have a distinct design that creates a flow of color throughout the quilt. The big blocks make this quilt fairly easy to put together. What color flowers will you create?

MATERIALS NEEDED

- See Fabric Requirements at right
- Rotary cutter
- Cutting mat
- Fabric scissors
- Fabric marking pen
- Needle
- Thread
- Pins
- Quilting ruler
- Batting

Before You Start

- Please read through the entire pattern first.
- The finished crib size quilt measures 48" x 48" (121.9 x 121.9cm); the finished throw size quilt measures 72" x 72" (182.9 x 182.9cm).
- The WOF is assumed to be 42" (106.7cm).
- The seam allowance is ¼" (6mm) unless otherwise noted.
- Unless otherwise stated, press the seams open or to the side you prefer.
- The backing yardage is based on 4" (10cm) overage on each side.
- Unit counts in parentheses in steps are separated with a comma for (crib, throw) quantities.
- SST = side-setting triangle
- CST = corner-setting triangle
- Share your quilt on Instagram using the hashtag #OrchidGardenQuilt.

FABRIC REQUIREMENTS

	Crib 48" x 48" (121.9 x 121.9cm)	Throw 72" x 72" (182.9 x 182.9cm)
Fabric 1	1 F8 or ¼ yd. (22.9cm)	1 FQ or ¼ yd. (22.9cm)
Fabric 2	1 FQ or ¼ yd. (22.9cm)	⅓ yd. (30.5cm)
Fabric 3	1 FQ or ¼ yd. (22.9cm)	1 FQ or ¼ yd. (22.9cm)
Fabric 4	1 FQ or ¼ yd. (22.9cm)	1 FQ or ¼ yd. (22.9cm)
Fabric 5	1 FQ or ¼ yd. (22.9cm)	1 FQ or ¼ yd. (22.9cm)
Fabric 6	1 FQ or ¼ yd. (22.9cm)	⅓ yd. (30.5cm)
Fabric 7	1 F8 or ¼ yd. (22.9cm)	1 FQ or ¼ yd. (22.9cm)
Fabric 8	–	1 FQ or ¼ yd. (22.9cm)
Fabric 9	–	1 FQ or ¼ yd. (22.9cm)
Fabric 10	–	⅓ yd. (30.5cm)
Fabric 11	–	1 FQ or ¼ yd. (22.9cm)
Background	1¾ yds. (1.6m)	3 yds. (2.7m)
Binding	½ yd. (45.7cm)	¾ yd. (68.6cm)
Backing	3¼ yds. (3m)	4½ yds. (4.1m)

Basic Block and Quilt Layout

- This quilt is made of several flower blocks turned "on point" at a 45-degree angle.

- Each flower block is made of four petal blocks.

- Instructions are given for how many of each color petal you will need and how many of each flower combination you will need.

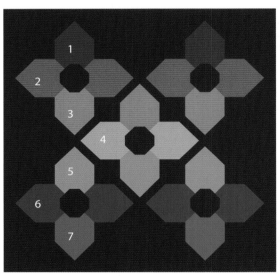

Flower Block
Turned on Point

CRIB SIZE	
Number of Petal Blocks	Crib Size Fabric
2	Fabrics 1, 4, and 7
3	Fabrics 3 and 5
4	Fabrics 2 and 6

THROW SIZE	
Number of Petal Blocks	Throw Size Fabric
3	Fabrics 1 and 11
4	Fabrics 4 and 8
5	Fabrics 3, 5, 7, and 9
6	Fabrics 2, 6, and 10

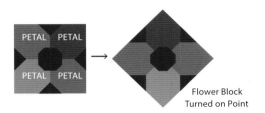

Crib Size Diagram

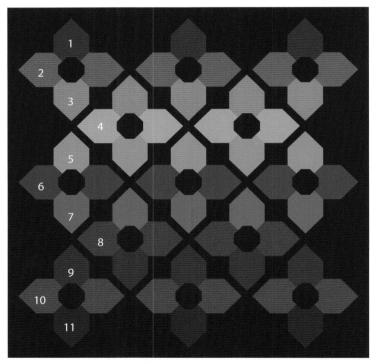

Throw Size Diagram

CUTTING INSTRUCTIONS PART 1

Crib 48" x 48" (121.9 x 121.9cm)	Throw 72" x 72" (182.9 x 182.9cm)	Cut from each fabric
Fabrics 1, 4, and 7		Two A 5½" x 5½" (14 x 14cm) Two B 3½" x 3½" (8.9 x 8.9cm) Two C 2" x 2" (5 x 5cm) Four D 3" x 3" (7.6 x 7.6cm)
Fabrics 3 and 5	Fabrics 1 and 11	Three A 5½" x 5½" (14 x 14cm) Three B 3½" x 3½" (8.9 x 8.9cm) Three C 2" x 2" (5 x 5cm) Six D 3" x 3" (7.6 x 7.6cm)
	Fabrics 4 and 8	Four A 5½" x 5½" (14 x 14cm) Four B 3½" x 3½" (8.9 x 8.9cm) Four C 2" x 2" (5 x 5cm) Eight D 3" x 3" (7.6 x 7.6cm)
Fabrics 2 and 6	Fabrics 3, 5, 7 and 9 (See suggested cutting diagram on page 122.)	Five A 5½" x 5½" (14 x 14cm) Five B 3½" x 3½" (8.9 x 8.9cm) Five C 2" x 2" (5 x 5cm) Ten D 3" x 3" (7.6 x 7.6cm)
	Fabrics 2, 6, and 10 (See suggested cutting diagram on page 122.)	Six A 5½" x 5½" (14 x 14cm) Six B 3½" x 3½" (8.9 x 8.9cm) Six C 2" x 2" (5 x 5cm) Twelve D 3" x 3" (7.6 x 7.6cm)

Choose a background fabric that will allow the colors of your finished blocks to pop.

CUTTING INSTRUCTIONS PART 2

	Crib 48" x 48" (121.9 x 121.9cm)	Throw 72" x 72" (182.9 x 182.9cm)
Background	Cut two 3½" (8.9cm) x WOF, Subcut: Twenty E 3½" x 3½" (8.9 x 8.9cm)	Cut five 3½" (8.9cm) x WOF, Subcut: Fifty-two E 3½" x 3½" (8.9 x 8.9cm)
	Cut one 17½" (44.5cm) x WOF, Subcut: Two F 17½" x 17½" (44.5 x 44.5cm)	Cut two 17½" (44.5cm) x WOF, Subcut: Four F 17½" x 17½" (44.5 x 44.5cm)
	Cut one 18½" (47cm) x WOF, Subcut: One G 18½" x 18½" (47 x 47cm)	Cut one 18½" (47cm) x WOF, Subcut: One G 18½" x 18½" (47 x 47cm)
	Cut one from remaining, Subcut: Twenty H 3" x 3" (7.6 x 7.6cm)	Cut one from remaining, Subcut: Fifty-two H 3" x 3" (7.6 x 7.6cm)
	Cut eight I 2" (5cm) x WOF	Cut seventeen I 2" (5cm) x WOF
	Set aside for sashing.	Set aside for sashing.

Suggested Cutting Diagrams

Most cutting is fairly straightforward, but the cutting for the following pieces in the throw-size quilt can be tricky. Please use these diagrams for suggested cutting.

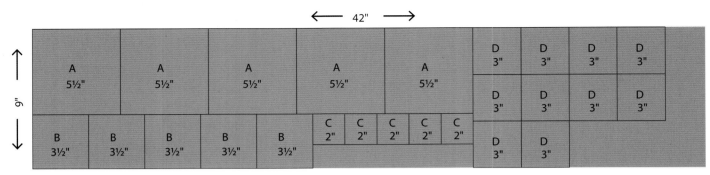

Throw Size: Fabrics 3, 5, 7, and 9

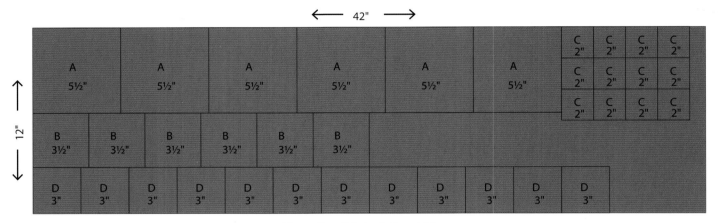

Throw Size: Fabrics 2, 6, and 10

Petal Blocks

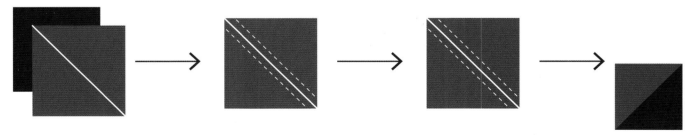

1. Each petal requires one pair of HSTs. For each HST pair, draw a diagonal line from corner to corner on the wrong side of each B piece. Align each B piece RST with an E piece. Sew a ¼" (6mm) seam on both sides of the drawn line. Then cut on the marked diagonal line, as shown in the diagram. Press the seams open and trim to 3" (7.6cm) square. Repeat this step for all B and E pieces. You should have (20, 52) pairs of HSTs.

2. Draw a diagonal line on the back of each C piece. Place one C piece RST on the top right corner of one H piece. Sew on the drawn line. Trim ¼" (6mm) from the seam and press the seam open. Repeat this step for all C and H pieces to create (20, 52) of these "stitch-n-flip" blocks.

HST pair   Stitch-n-Flip
                    Block

3. For each petal block, gather one HST pair, one stitch-n-flip block, one A piece, and two D pieces of the same color.

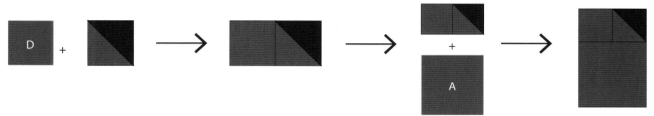

4. Sew one D piece to the left side of one HST as shown. Note the orientation of the blocks in the diagram. Press the seam open, then sew these to the top of the A piece. Press the seam.

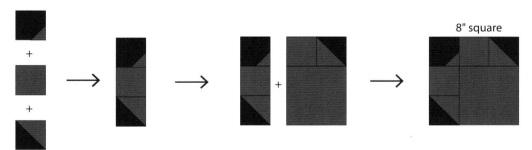

8" square

5. Sew the stitch-n-flip block to the top of the C piece and sew the other HST to the bottom of the C piece, as shown in the diagram. Press the seams open. Sew this section to the left of the Step 4 section and press the seam.

6. Repeat Steps 3–5 to make all (20, 52) petal blocks. (Refer to the quilt layouts on pages 125–126 to confirm you have the correct number of petals for each fabric.)

Flower Assembly

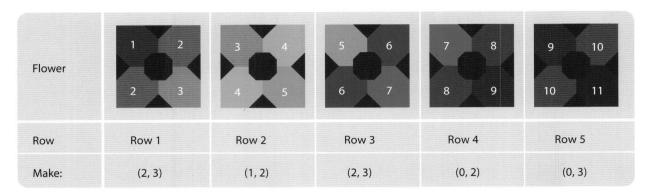

Flower					
Row	Row 1	Row 2	Row 3	Row 4	Row 5
Make:	(2, 3)	(1, 2)	(2, 3)	(0, 2)	(0, 3)

1. Each flower is created from four petal blocks. Check the chart above to see how many of each flower to create.

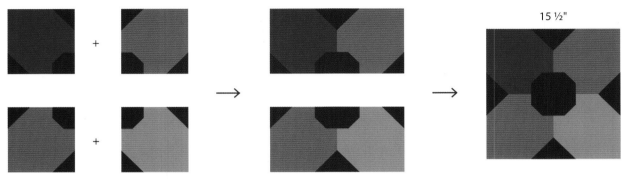

2. Gather the four petal blocks needed for each flower. Sew the top two blocks together and the bottom two blocks together to create two rows, as shown in the diagram. Press the seams as you go, then sew the two rows together and press. Repeat this step to create all (5, 13) flower blocks.

Setting Pieces

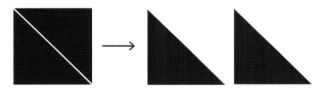

1. Cut on the diagonal of each F piece to create two SSTs. You should have a total of (4, 8) SSTs.

2. Cut on the diagonal of each G piece in each direction to create four CSTs.

(8, 18) 2" x 15 ½" strips

(2, 2) 2" x 18 ½" strips

(2, 2) 2" x 51 ½" strips

(0, 2) 2" x 84 ½" strips

3. From (4, 9) I pieces, cut (8, 18) 2" x 15½" (5 x 39.4cm) strips. From one I piece, cut two 2" x 18½" (5 x 47cm) strips. Sew the remaining (3, 7) I pieces end to end. Press the seams open. From this long strip, cut two 2" x 51½" (5 x 130.8cm) strips and (0, 2) 2" x 84½" (5 x 214.6cm) strips for the sashing.

Note: From here, go to either Quilt Assembly—Crib Size or Quilt Assembly—Throw Size, depending on the size you are making, and follow the steps.

Quilt Assembly—Crib Size

This quilt is sewn "on point," meaning the blocks are arranged on the diagonal. Begin by arranging all of your blocks according to the diagram. Press toward the sashing strips throughout these steps.

1. Sew each row on the diagonal. Sew a 2" x 15½" (5 x 39.4cm) sashing strip between each block and on the end of each row, as shown in the diagram. Press the seams as you go.

2. Sew a 2" x 18½" (5 x 47cm) sashing strip to the top of Row 1 and the bottom of Row 3. Then sew a 2" x 51½" (5 x 130.8cm) sashing strip to both sides of Row 2.

3. Sew an SST to each end of Rows 1 and 3. Press toward the triangles. Sew a CST to each end of Row 2. Press toward the triangles.

4. Finish by sewing each row together. Add the final CSTs to the top left corner and bottom right corner. Press toward the sashing as you go.

Note: SSTs and CSTs are designed to have a slight amount of overage to allow for a ¼" (6mm) seam along the edges. To reduce bulk, you may trim the dog-ears to be even with the sashing as you press these blocks.

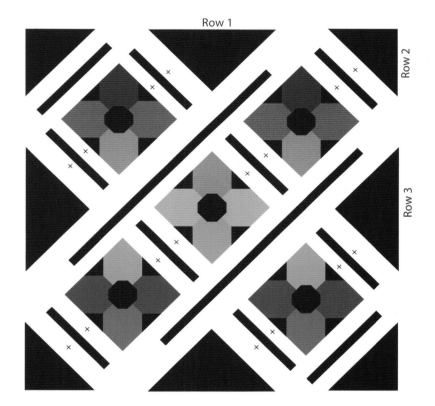

Crib Size Layout Diagram

Quilt Assembly—Throw Size

This quilt is sewn "on point," meaning the blocks are arranged on the diagonal. Begin by arranging all of your blocks according to the diagram. Press toward the sashing strips throughout these steps.

1. Sew each row on the diagonal. Sew a 2" x 15½" (5 x 39.4cm) sashing strip between each block and on the end of each row, as shown in the diagram. Press the seams as you go.

2. Sew a 2" x 18½" (5 x 47cm) sashing strip to the top of Row 1 and the bottom of Row 5. Then sew a 2" x 51½" (5 x 130.8cm) sashing strip to the top of Row 2 and the bottom of Row 4.

3. Sew a 2" x 84½" (5 x 214.6cm) sashing strip to both sides of Row 3.

4. Sew an SST to each end of Rows 1, 2, 4, and 5. Press toward the triangles. Sew a CST to each end of Row 3. Press toward the triangles.

5. Finish by sewing each row together. Add the final CSTs to the top left corner and bottom right corner. Press toward the sashing as you go.

Note: SSTs and CSTs are designed to have a slight amount of overage to allow for a ¼" (6mm) seam along the edges. To reduce bulk, you may trim the dog-ears to be even with the sashing as you press these blocks.

Throw Size Layout Diagram

Because this quilt uses solid colors, the quilting really stands out as an important element of the finished piece.

Pumpkin Roll

By Kiley Ferons of Kiley's Quilting Room

I know this pattern has the word "pumpkin" in it, but you can make it whatever fruit or vegetable you want. Apple, kiwi, lemon, etc.—you choose! Regardless, this has long been a fan-favorite quilt pattern that bridges the gap between the modern and traditional worlds of quilting. Hone your curve-piecing skills and incorporate the traditional sawtooth star to create a block that will make a statement wherever you display this quilt.

MATERIALS NEEDED

- See Fabric Requirements (page 130)
- Rotary cutter
- Cutting mat
- Fabric scissors
- Fabric marking pen
- Needle
- Thread
- Pins
- Quilting ruler
- Batting

Before You Start

- Read through all of the instructions first.
- The finished size of the quilt is 54" x 66" (137.2 x 167.6cm).
- The WOF is assumed to be 42" (106.7cm).
- The seam allowance is ¼" (6mm) unless otherwise noted.
- Print the templates at 100 percent, not "fit to page." Measure the 1" (2.5cm) reference square on your printout to ensure that everything is the correct size.
- When posting online or searching for ideas for your quilt, use or search the hashtag #PumpkinRollQuilt.

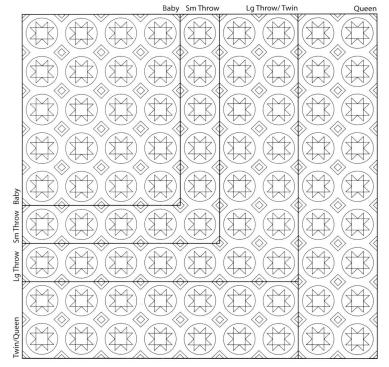

Copy and color in the black-and-white diagram to test different color arrangements before you cut!

I have laid out the fabric requirements and cutting instructions for two colors. If you want a "scrappier" or "mix-of-fabrics" look, follow the "1 Block" instructions for the colors, and follow the background and accent instructions for the size you are making.

FABRIC REQUIREMENTS

	1 Block	Baby	Small Throw	Large Throw	Twin	Queen
	10" x 10" (25.4 x 25.4cm)	40" x 50" (101.6 x 127cm)	50" x 60" (127 x 152.4cm)	70" x 70" (177.8 x 177.8cm)	70" x 90" (177.8 x 228.6cm)	90" x 90" (228.6 x 228.6cm)
Color 1	1 FQ	1 yd. (90cm)	1¾ yds. (1.6m)	2¼ yds. (2.1m)	2¾ yds. (2.5m)	3¾ yds. (3.4m)
Color 2	1 FQ	1 yd. (90cm)	1¾ yds. (1.6m)	2¼ yds. (2.1m)	2¾ yds. (2.5m)	3¾ yds. (3.4m)
Background	1 FQ	2¾ yds. (2.5m)	4 yds. (3.7m)	6½ yds. (5.9m)	8¼ yds. (7.5m)	10½ yds. (9.6m)
Accent Color	5" x 5" (12.7 x 12.7cm)	½ yd. (45.7cm)	¾ yd. (68.6cm)	1 yd. (90cm)	1¼ yds. (1.1m)	1½ yds. (1.4m)
Backing		2¾ yds. (2.5m)	3¼ yds. (3m)	4½ yds. (4.1m)	6½ yds. (5.9m)	8½ yds. (7.8m)
Binding		½ yd. (45.7cm)	½ yd. (45.7cm)	½ yd. (45.7cm)	¾ yd. (68.6cm)	¾ yd. (68.6cm)

CUTTING INSTRUCTIONS

	1 Block	Baby	Small Throw	Large Throw	Twin	Queen
Color 1 and Color 2	Only 1 color Two 1¾" x 6½" (4.5 x 16.5cm) Two 1¾" x 9" (4.5 x 22.9cm) Four 2" x 2" (5 x 5cm) One 3½" x 3½" (8.9 x 8.9cm) One 6" x 6" (15.2 x 15.2cm)	Two 6" (15.2cm) x WOF, Subcut: Ten 6" x 6" (15.2 x 15.2cm) Six 3½" x 3½" (8.9 x 8.9cm)	Two 6" (15.2cm) x WOF, Subcut: Fourteen 6" x 6" (15.2 x 15.2cm)	Four 6" (15.2cm) x WOF, Subcut: Twenty-five 6" x 6" (15.2 x 15.2cm) Five 3½" x 3½" (8.9 x 8.9cm)	Five 6" (15.2cm) x WOF, Subcut: Thirty-two 6" x 6" (15.2 x 15.2cm)	Six 6" (15.2cm) x WOF, Subcut: Forty-one 6" x 6" (15.2 x 15.2cm)
		One 3½" (8.9cm) x WOF, Subcut: Four 3½" x 3½" (8.9 x 8.9cm) Fourteen 2" x 2" (5 x 5cm)	Two 3½" (8.9cm) x WOF, Subcut: Fifteen 3½" x 3½" (8.9 x 8.9cm) Fourteen 2" x 2" (5 x 5cm)	Two 3½" (8.9cm) x WOF, Subcut: Twenty 3½" x 3½" (8.9 x 8.9cm)	Three 3½" (8.9cm) x WOF, Subcut: Thirty-two 3½" x 3½" (8.9 x 8.9cm)	Four 3½" (8.9cm) x WOF, Subcut: Forty-one 3½" x 3½" (8.9 x 8.9cm)
		One 2" (5cm) x WOF, Subcut: Twenty-one 2" x 2" (5 x 5cm)	One 2" (5cm) x WOF, Subcut: Forty-six 2" x 2" (5 x 5cm)	Five 2" (5cm) x WOF, Subcut: One hundred 2" x 2" (5 x 5cm)	Seven 2" (5cm) x WOF, Subcut: One hundred twenty-eight 2" x 2" (5 x 5cm)	Eight 2" (5cm) x WOF, Subcut: One hundred sixty-four 2" x 2" (5 x 5cm)
		One 9" (22.9cm) x WOF, Subcut: Twenty 9" x 1¾" (22.9 x 4.5cm) Five 2" x 2" (5 x 5cm)	Two 9" (22.9cm) x WOF, Subcut: Thirty 9" x 1¾" (22.9 x 4.5cm) One 6" x 6" (15.2 x 15.2cm)	Three 9" (22.9cm) x WOF, Subcut: Fifty 9" x 1¾" (22.9 x 4.5cm) Twenty-two 6½" x 1¾" (16.5 x 4.5cm)	Three 9" (22.9cm) x WOF, Subcut: Sixty-four 9" x 1¾" (22.9 x 4.5cm)	Four 9" (22.9cm) x WOF, Subcut: Eighty-two 9" x 1¾" (22.9 x 4.5cm)
		One 6½" (16.5cm) x WOF, Subcut: Twenty 6½" x 1¾" (16.5 x 4.5cm)	Two 6½" (16.5cm) x WOF, Subcut: Thirty 6½" x 1¾" (16.5 x 4.5cm)	Two 6½" (16.5cm) x WOF, Subcut: Twenty-eight 6½" x 1¾" (16.5 x 4.5cm)	Three 6½" (16.5cm) x WOF, Subcut: Sixty-four 6½" x 1¾" (16.5 x 4.5cm)	Four 6½" (16.5cm) x WOF, Subcut: Eighty-two 6½" x 1¾" (16.5 x 4.5cm)

Background	Four 1½" x 1½" (4 x 4cm) One 6" x 6" (15.2 x 15.2cm) One 11" x 11" (27.9 x 27.9cm)	Seven 11" (27.9cm) x WOF, Subcut: Twenty 11" x 11" (27.9 x 27.9cm) Seven 6" x 6" (15.2 x 15.2cm)	Ten 11" (27.9cm) x WOF, Subcut: Thirty 11" x 11" (27.9 x 27.9cm) Ten 6" x 6" (15.2 x 15.2cm)	Seventeen 11" (27.9cm) x WOF, Subcut: Fifty 11" x 11" (27.9 x 27.9cm) Seventeen 6" x 6" (15.2 x 15.2cm)	Twenty-two 11" (27.9cm) x WOF, Subcut: Sixty-four 11" x 11" (27.9 x 27.9cm) Twenty-two 6" x 6" (15.2 x 15.2cm)	Twenty-eight 11" (27.9cm) x WOF, Subcut: Eighty-two 11" x 11" (27.9 x 27.9cm) Twenty-eight 6" x 6" (15.2 x 15.2cm)
		Two 6" (15.2cm) x WOF Subcut: Thirteen 6" x 6" (15.2 x 15.2cm)	Three 6" (15.2cm) x WOF Subcut: Twenty 6" x 6" (15.2 x 15.2cm)	Five 6" (15.2cm) x WOF Subcut: Thirty-three 6" x 6" (15.2 x 15.2cm)	Six 6" (15.2cm) x WOF Subcut: Forty-two 6" x 6" (15.2 x 15.2cm)	Eight 6" (15.2cm) x WOF Subcut: Fifty-four 6" x 6" (15.2 x 15.2cm)
		Three 1½" (4cm) x WOF, Subcut: Eighty 1½" x 1½" (4 x 4cm)	Five 1½" (4cm) x WOF, Subcut: One hundred twenty 1½" x 1½" (4 x 4cm)	Eight 1½" (4cm) x WOF, Subcut: Two hundred 1½" x 1½" (4 x 4cm)	Ten 1½" (4cm) x WOF, Subcut: Two hundred fifty-six 1½" x 1½" (4 x 4cm)	Twelve 1½" (4cm) x WOF, Subcut: Three hundred twenty-eight 1½" x 1½" (4 x 4cm)
Accent	Four 2½" x 2½" (6 x 6cm)	Five 2½" (6cm) x WOF, Subcut: Eighty 2½" x 2½" (6 x 6cm)	Eight 2½" (6cm) x WOF, Subcut: One hundred twenty 2½" x 2½" (6 x 6cm)	Thirteen 2½" (6cm) x WOF, Subcut: Two hundred 2½" x 2½" (6 x 6cm)	Sixteen 2½" (6cm) x WOF, Subcut: Two hundred fifty-six 2½" x 2½" (6 x 6cm)	Twenty-one 2½" (6cm) x WOF, Subcut: Three hundred twenty-eight 2½" x 2½" (6 x 6cm)

This project pairs traditional quilt designs with sophisticated color combinations to create a fresh style.

Making the Star Block

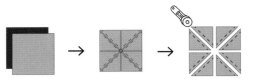

(x8)

Trim to 2"

1. Place a 6" x 6" (15.2 x 15.2cm) background piece RST with each of the 6" x 6" (15.2 x 15.2cm) Color 1 and Color 2 pieces. On the back of the lighter fabric square in each pair, draw two diagonal lines and two perpendicular lines through the center, as shown in the diagram. Sew on both sides of both diagonal lines only, then cut on each line. Open up your eight HSTs and press to the darker side. Trim each one to 2" (5cm) square.

Row 1   Row 2

2. Sew a row comprising a 2" x 2" (5 x 5cm) Color 1 piece, a Color 1 HST, another Color 1 HST, and another 2" x 2" (5 x 5cm) Color 1 piece, as shown. Press as desired. Repeat with the 2" x 2" (5 x 5cm) Color 2 pieces and Color 2 HSTs. Then sew two HSTs together, as shown. Repeat to create two of each of these rows per block that you are making.

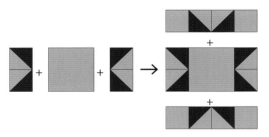

3. Sew a Color 1 Row 2 on both sides of a 3½" x 3½" (8.9 x 8.9cm) Color 1 piece. Press the seams open. Then sew a Color 1 Row 1 to the top and bottom. Press the seams open. Do the same thing with the Color 2 rows and pieces.

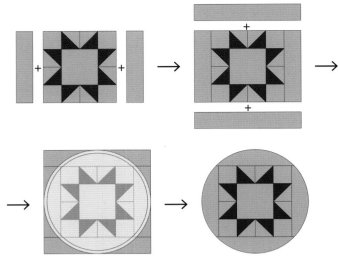

4. Sew a 1¾" x 6½" (4.5 x 16.5cm) Color 1 piece to both sides of the unit from Step 3. Press the seams to one side. Sew a 1¾" x 9" (4.5 x 22.9cm) Color 1 piece to the top and bottom. Press the seams. Do the same thing with the Color 2 blocks and pieces. Center the inner circle template on your star blocks. Cut around the template and keep the circles.

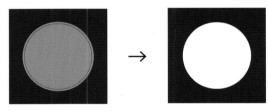

5. Place the background circle template in the center of all the 11" x 11" (27.9 x 27.9cm) background pieces and cut around the template. Discard the circles and keep the "frame" pieces.

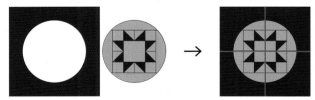

6. Take one inner circle piece and one frame piece. Fold each one in half, then in half again to create creases. Lay the frame on top of the inner circle, both pieces right side up, aligning the creases in the fabrics.

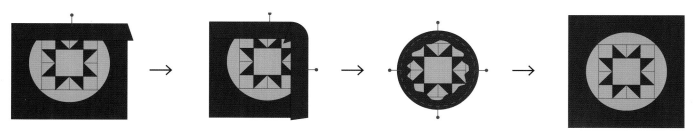

7. Beginning with the top edge of the frame piece, pull the edge down toward the center until the edge of both curves are aligned (now they are RST). Pin in place where the creases match. Repeat on all sides on the creases. The entire frame should now be facing down. Sew a ¼" (6mm) around the circle, aligning the edges as you go. Press toward the center. Repeat Steps 6 and 7 with all remaining inner circles and frame pieces.

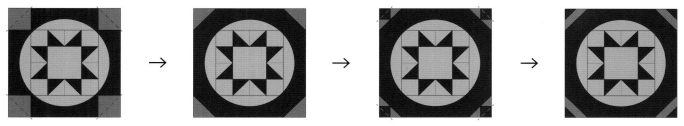

8. Draw a diagonal line on the backs of all 2¼" (5.7cm) accent squares and 1½" (4cm) background squares. Place one 2½" (6cm) accent square, RST, on each corner of every block, aligned as shown in the diagram, and sew on the diagonal line. Press and cut ¼" (6mm) away from the sewn line. Repeat this with the 1½" (4cm) background squares, as shown in the diagram.

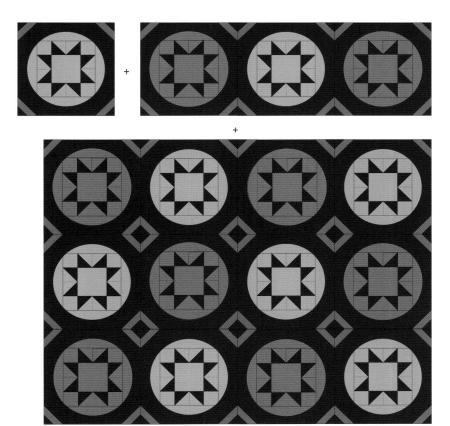

9. You should have ten of each colored block for the baby size, fifteen of each colored block for the small throw, twenty-four of each colored block for the large throw (one block will not be used), thirty-two of each colored block for the twin size (one block will not be used), and forty-one of each colored block for the queen size (one block will not be used).

10. Arrange your blocks as desired and sew them into rows. Press the seams in each row to the opposite direction as the row before it so the seams will nest. Then sew all the rows together and press.

11. Quilt and bind as desired.

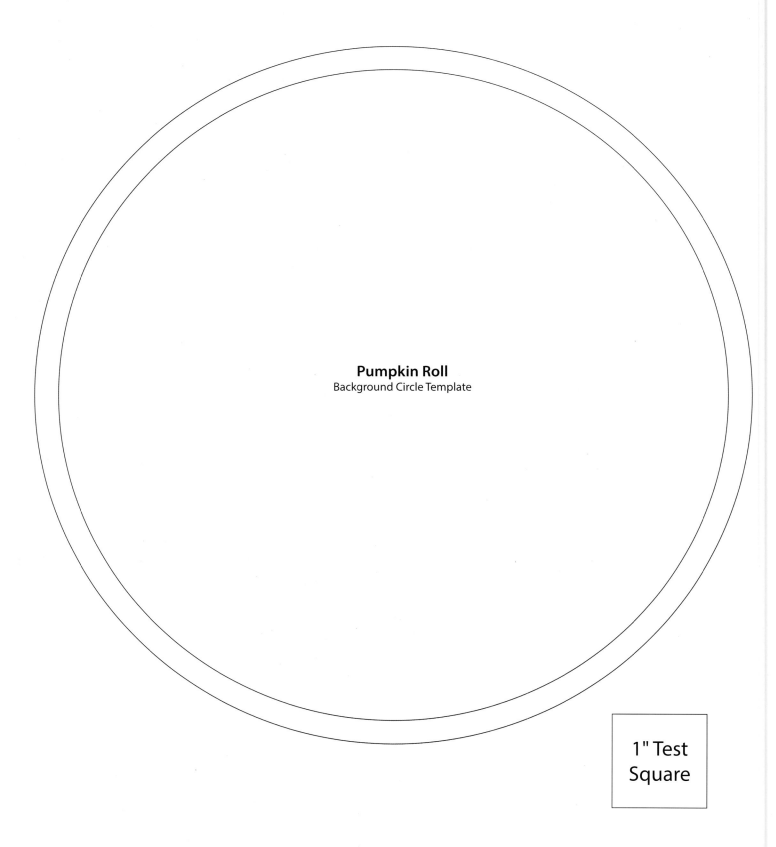

Pumpkin Roll
Background Circle Template

1" Test
Square

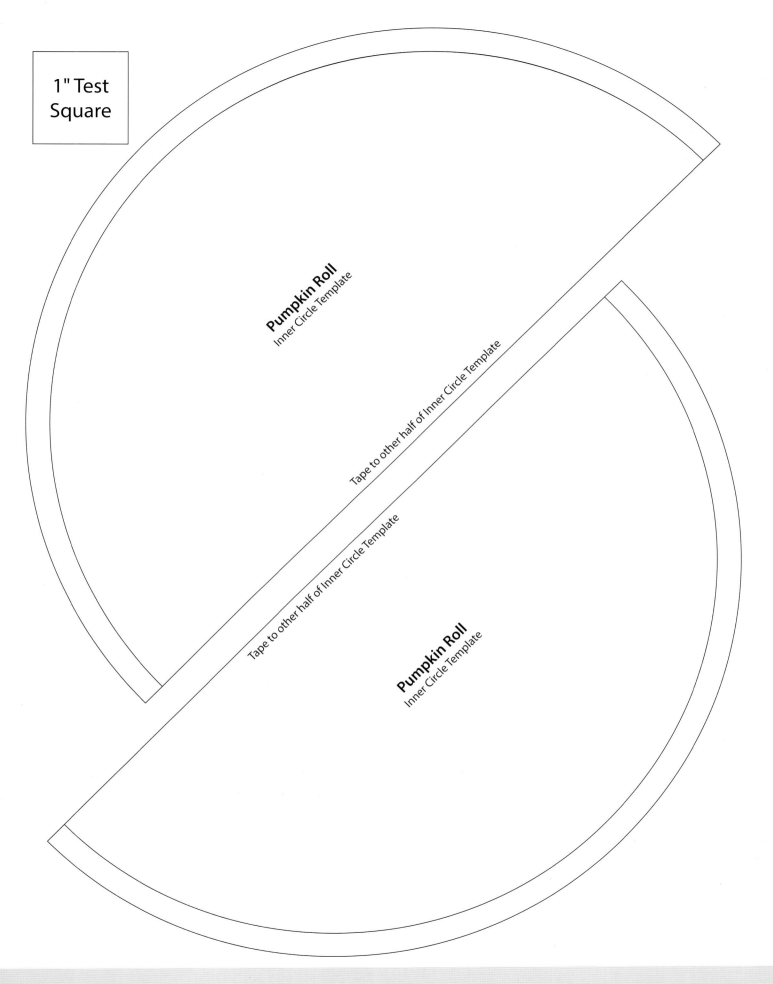

1" Test
Square

Pumpkin Roll
Inner Circle Template

Tape to other half of Inner Circle Template

Tape to other half of Inner Circle Template

Pumpkin Roll
Inner Circle Template

Riverbend

By Kiley Ferons of Kiley's Quilting Room

This advanced pattern is stunning but tricky. Be sure to try out these curves on a practice block before moving on to the rest of the quilt. Even though it's tricky, it is still doable and a great way to increase your skills and practice. Be sure to starch your fabrics to help avoid stretching and warping.

MATERIALS NEEDED

- See Fabric Requirements at right
- Rotary cutter
- Cutting mat
- Fabric scissors
- Fabric marking pen
- Needle
- Thread
- Pins
- Quilting ruler
- Batting

Before You Start

- The size of the finished quilt is 57½" x 57½" (146.1 x 146.1cm).
- Print templates at 100 percent, not "fit to page." Measure the 1" (2.5cm) reference square on your printout to ensure that everything is the correct size.
- The seam allowance is ¼" (6mm) unless otherwise noted. The precision of the seam allowance is very important for this pattern. Plan to test one block first to make sure the sizing is correct. If not, adjust your seam allowance accordingly.
- Use starch to avoid warping and to help with precision.
- Share your quilt on Instagram using the hashtag #RiverbendQuilt.

FABRIC REQUIREMENTS

Fabric	Measurements
White	3¼ yds. (3m)
Black	4 yds. (3.7m)
Backing	3¾ yds. (3.4m)
Binding	½ yd. (45.7cm)

CUTTING INSTRUCTIONS

White	Black
Four 5½" (14cm) x WOF, Subcut: Forty-eight Template 2s	Five 7½" (19.1cm) x WOF, Subcut: Fifty Template 5s Eight Template 3s
Five 7" (17.8cm) x WOF, Subcut: Fifty Template 4s	Three 6" (15.2cm) x WOF, Subcut: Forty-two Template 3s
Six 8½" x WOF, Subcut: Fifty Template 6s Two Template 2s	Five 12½" (31.8cm) x WOF, Subcut: Twenty-five Template 7s From the remaining amounts and scraps, cut: Twenty Template 1s
	Three 4½" (11.4cm) x WOF, Subcut: Thirty Template 1s

Note: Suggested cutting layouts are on page 138.

Copy and color in the black-and-white diagram to test different color arrangements before you cut!

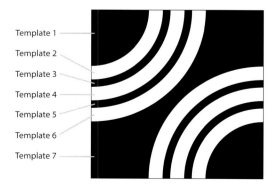

Template 1
Template 2
Template 3
Template 4
Template 5
Template 6
Template 7

12" x 12"

Suggested Cutting Layouts

- Cut twelve Template 2s from each of the four 5½" (14cm) x WOF strips of white.

- Cut ten Template 4s from each of the five 7" (17.8cm) x WOF strips of white.

- Cut nine Template 6s from each of five 8½" (21.6cm) x WOF strips of white. With the remaining 8½" (21.6cm) x WOF strip, cut five more Template 6s and two more Template 2s.

- Cut eleven Template 5s from each of four 7½" (19.1cm) x WOF strips of black. With the remaining 7½" (19.1cm) x WOF strip, cut six more Template 5s and eight Template 3s.

- Cut fourteen Template 3s from each of the three 6" (15.2cm) x WOF strips of black.

- Cut six Template 7s and two Template 1s from each of four 12½" (31.8cm) x WOF strips of black. With the remaining 12½" (31.8cm) x WOF strip, cut one Template 7 and twelve Template 1s.

- Cut ten Template 1s from each of the three 4½" (11.4cm) x WOF strips of black.

Block Assembly

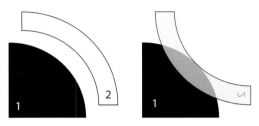

1. Take a #1 piece and lay it face up. Lay a #2 piece down along the curve, face up. Then flip the #2 piece face down so the top of both curves are aligned. Pin the centers together and then the edges. Sew along the curve and press toward the center.

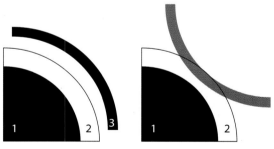

2. Lay a #3 piece down along the curve, face up. Then flip the #3 piece face down so the top of both curves are aligned. Pin the centers together and then the edges. Sew along the curve and press toward the center, being careful not to warp the fabric.

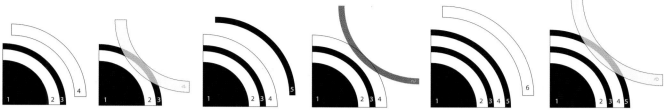

3. Repeat these steps, adding the rest of the numbered pieces in order through #6. Press the seams in toward #1. Do this entire process 50 times. Each completed quarter-circle block should measure 8½" (21.6cm) on each straight side. If it is measuring too big, increase your seam allowance.

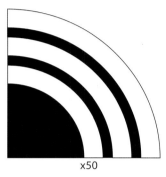

x50

4. Once your quarter-circles are complete, trim them to be squared from the right angle of piece #1.

5. Lay a #7 piece face up and lay one of the quarter-circle pieces face up, with the curves aligned. Flip the quarter-circle piece face down so the tops of both curves are aligned. Pin the centers together and then the edges. Sew along the curve and press toward the quarter-circle piece. Do the same for the other side of the #7 piece. Make twenty-five of these blocks. Trim your blocks to 12"x 12" (30.5x 30.5cm).

Quilt Top Assembly

1. Arrange your blocks as shown in the diagram. Sew the blocks into rows first. Press the seams in each row in the opposite direction as the row above it. Then sew the rows together and press your seams.

2. Quilt and bind as desired.

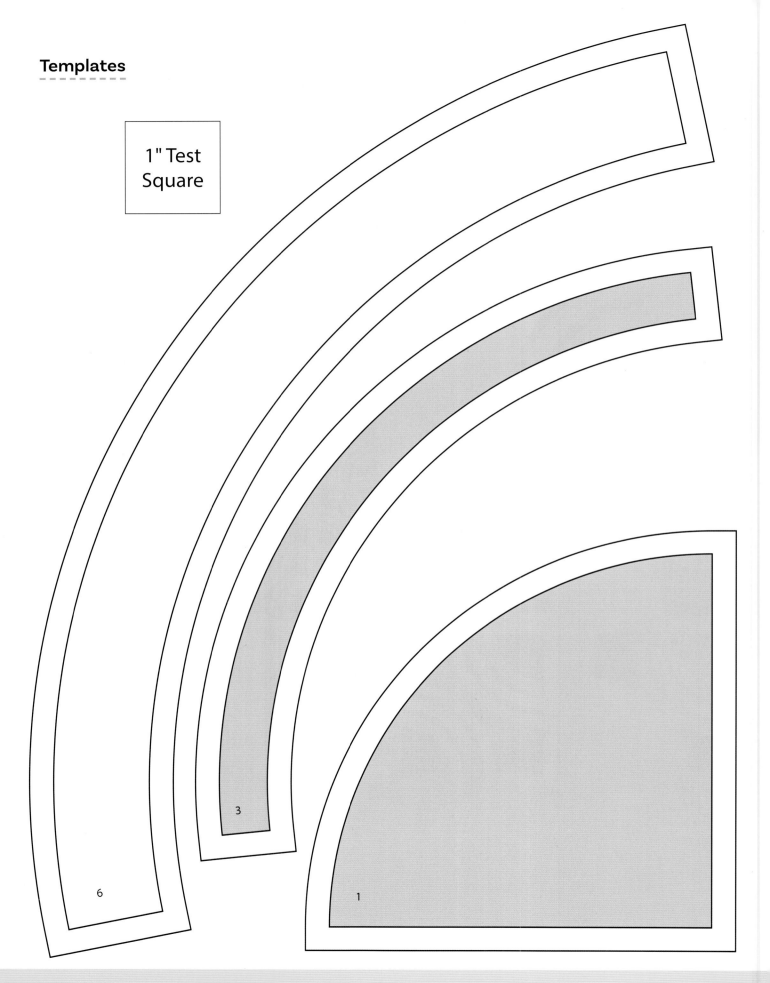

1" Test Square

3

6

1

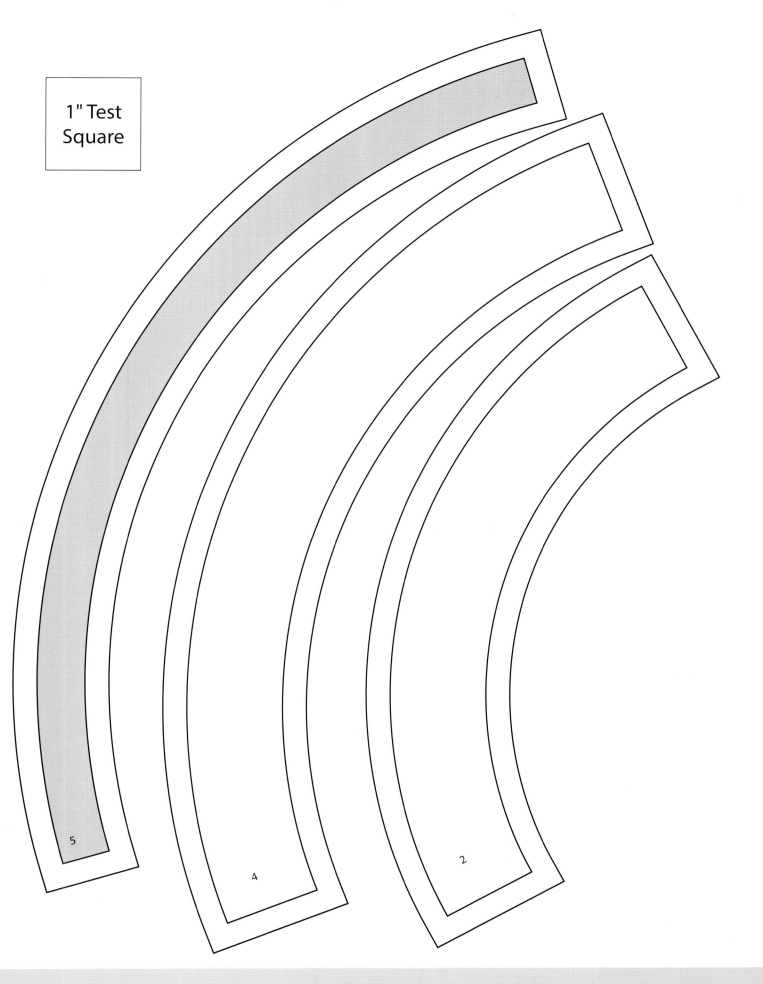

1" Test
Square

5

4

2

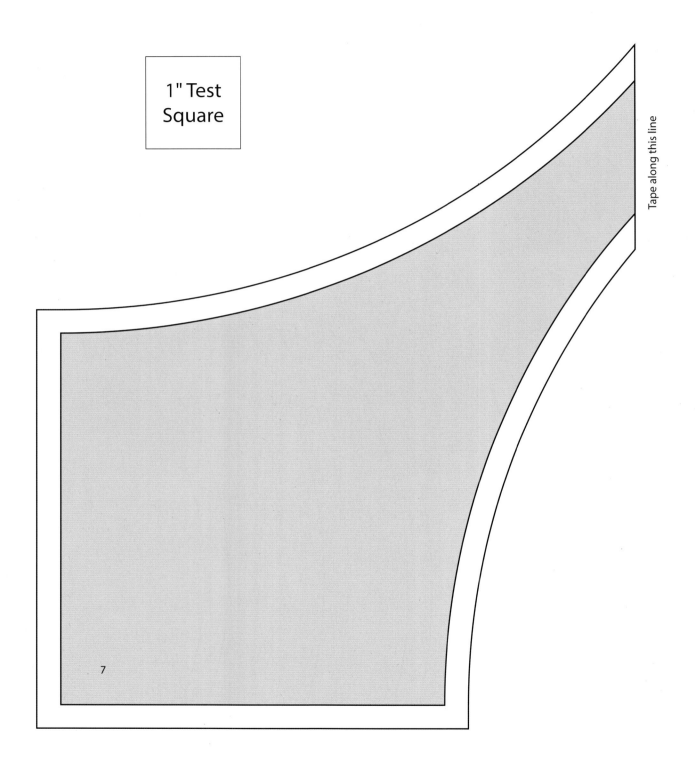

1" Test
Square

Tape along this line

7

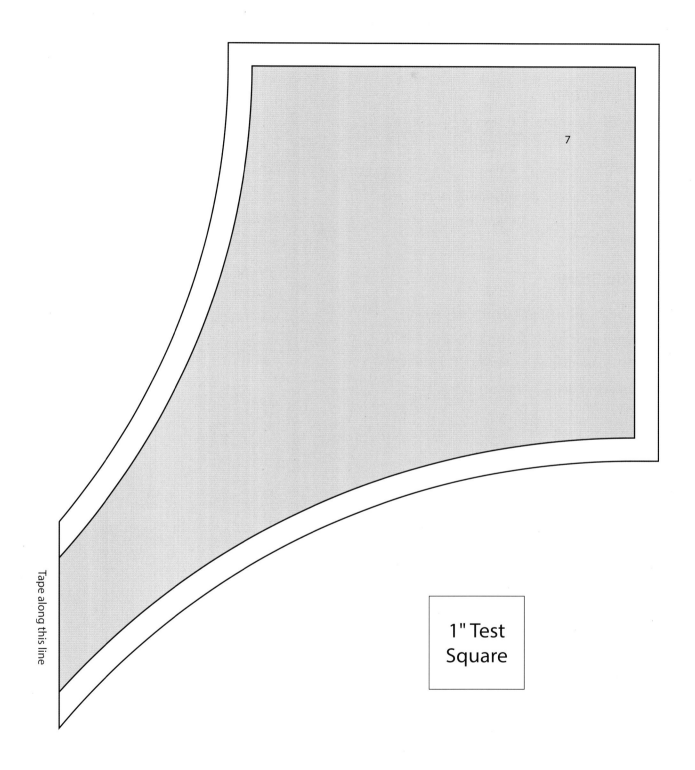

7

Tape along this line

1" Test
Square

Wandering

By Elza McKenna of Rippey Street Quilts

This pattern really keeps your eye moving across the design as you follow the flow of the lines. I love how it mimics the ebb and flow of sewing and quilting. It's like telling a story—a story that you can put on display for others to see and wonder about. True art makes us feel! This statement quilt is sure to make you feel something.

MATERIALS NEEDED

- See Fabric Requirements at right
- Rotary cutter
- Cutting mat
- Fabric scissors
- Fabric marking pen
- Needle
- Thread
- Pins
- Quilting ruler
- Batting

Before You Start

- Please read all instructions thoroughly first.
- The finished quilt size is 55" x 65" (139.7 x 165.1cm).
- The WOF is assumed to be 44"–45" (111.8–114.3cm).
- The seam allowance is ¼" (6mm) unless otherwise noted.

FABRIC REQUIREMENTS

Fabric	Measurements
Primary Color	1½ yds. (1.4m)
Circle Color	¼ yd. (22.9cm)
Accent Color 1	⅛ yd. (11.4cm)
Accent Color 2	⅛ yd. (11.4cm)
Accent Color 3	⅛ yd. (11.4cm)
Background	2½ yds. (2.3m)
Backing	3½ yds. (3.2m)
Binding	½ yd. (45.7cm)

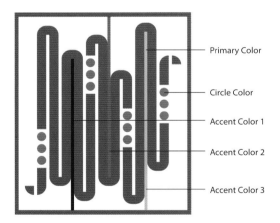

— Primary Color
— Circle Color
— Accent Color 1
— Accent Color 2
— Accent Color 3

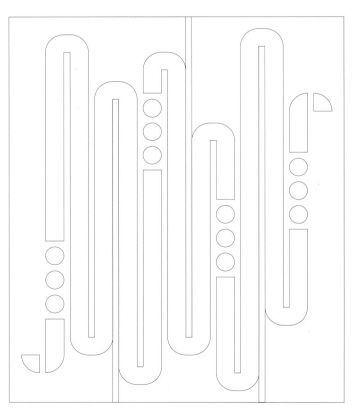

Copy and color in the black-and-white diagram to test different color arrangements before you cut!

This design looks amazing no matter how it's oriented.

CUTTING INSTRUCTIONS

Fabric	Measurement
Primary Color	Cut eight 3½" x 54" (8.9 x 190.5cm), Subcut: One 3½" x 48½" (8.9 x 123.2cm) Two 3½" x 45½" (8.9 x 115.8cm) One 3½" x 44½" (8.9 x 113cm) One 3½" x 40½" (8.9 x 102.9cm) Two 3½" x 33½" (8.9 x 85.1cm) One 3½" x 32½" (8.9 x 82.6cm) One 3½" x 16½" (8.9 x 41.9cm) One 3½" x 13½" (8.9 x 34.3cm) One 3½" x 10½" (8.9 x 26.7cm) One 3½" x 7½" (8.9 x 19.1cm) One 3½" x 6½" (8.9 x 16.5cm) One 3½" x 4½" (8.9 x 11.4cm)
Primary Color	Cut two 3¾" x 54" (9.5 x 190.5cm), Subcut: Twenty-four 3¾" x 3¾" (9.5 x 9.5cm) Ten 3½" x 1½" (8.9 x 4cm)
Circle Color	Cut two 3½" (8.9cm) x WOF, Subcut: Twenty-four 3½" x 2¼" (8.9 x 5.7cm)
Accent Color 1	Cut two 1½" (4cm) x WOF
Accent Color 2	Cut two 1½" (4cm) x WOF
Accent Color 3	Cut two 1½" (4cm) x WOF
Background	Cut three 3½" x 90" (8.9 x 228.6cm), Subcut: Two 3½" x 18½" (8.9 x 47cm) Two 3½" x 13½" (8.9 x 34.3cm) Two 3½" x 11½" (8.9 x 29.2cm) Four 3½" x 8½" (8.9 x 21.6cm) Two 3½" x 6½" (8.9 x 16.5cm) Four 3½" x 3½" (8.9 x 8.9cm) Six 3½" x 2½" (8.9 x 6cm) Twenty 3½" x 1½" (8.9 x 4cm)
Background	Cut seven 1½" x 90" (4 x 228.6cm), Subcut: One 1½" x 60½" (4 x 153.7cm) Two 1½" x 59½" (4 x 151.1cm) One 1½" x 56½" (4 x 143.5cm) One 1½" x 54½" (4 x 138.4cm) One 1½" x 49½" (4 x 125.7cm) One 1½" x 44½" (4 x 113cm) One 1½" x 18½" (4 x 47cm) One 1½" x 13½" (4 x 34.3cm) One 1½" x 11½" (4 x 29.2cm) Two 1½" x 8½" (4 x 21.6cm) One 1½" x 6½" (4 x 16.5cm) Two 1½" x 2½" (4 x 6cm)
Background	Cut one 9½" x 90" (24.1 x 228.6cm), Subcut: One 9½" x 13½" (24.1 x 34.3cm) One 9½" x 5½" (24.1 x 14cm) Twenty-four 4" x 4" (10 x 10cm)
Background	Cut two 6½" x 90" (16.5 x 228.6cm), Subcut: One 6½" x 57½" (16.5 x 146.1cm) One 6½" x 49½" (16.5 x 125.7cm) Twenty-four 2¼" x 4" (5.7 x 10cm)

A NOTE ABOUT CUTTING LONG STRIPS

Although it may be more difficult to manage, cutting fabric on the lengthwise grain will provide more stability to your quilt and prevent you from creating excess seams. It's especially useful for quilts like this one with long pieces of sashing. I fold my fabric in half twice with the selvage edges together and cut through four layers of fabric. This allows all my fabric to fit on my cutting mat. Be sure to change your rotary blade often; the sharper the better when cutting through layers!

Prepping Strips

1. Trace and cut Template B from twenty-four 4" x 4" (10 x 10cm) background fabric squares.

2. Trace and cut Template D from twenty-four 2¼" x 4" (5.7 x 10cm) background fabric pieces.

3. Trace and cut Template A from twenty-four 3¾" (9.5cm) main color squares.

4. Trace and cut Template C from twenty-four 3½" x 2¼" (8.9 x 5.7cm) circle color pieces.

5. Piece the remaining two 3½" x 54" (8.9 x 137.2cm) main color strips together using a diagonal seam and trim to 55½" (141cm).

6. Piece all 1½" (4cm) Accent Color 1 strips together end to end using a diagonal seam and trim to 51½" (130.8cm).

7. Piece all 1½" (4cm) Accent Color 2 strips together end to end using a diagonal seam and trim to 54½" (138.4cm).

8. Piece all 1½" (4cm) Accent Color 3 strips together end to end using a diagonal seam and trim to 60½" (153.7cm).

No-Pin Method

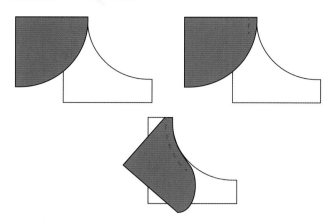

1. With RST, place Template A on top of Template B as shown in the diagram. Then, using a ¼" (6mm) seam, take a few stitches to stabilize the edge of the curve.

2. Sewing slowly, gently guide the edges of Templates A and B together under your presser foot and sew until you reach the end of the curve. Continue to keep the edges of your fabric aligned along a ¼" (6mm) seam the whole time. The fabric may begin to pucker slightly as you guide it together.

3. Press the seam toward the main color fabric. Don't worry if the edges do not align perfectly, as you will trim these blocks down. This method takes time and practice to master. Keep at it!

Quarter-Circle Blocks

1. Gather twenty-four Template A pieces and twenty-four Template B pieces. Sew them together to create twenty-four units. I prefer to sew curves using the No-Pin Method above, but use your favorite method for sewing curves.

Half-Circle Blocks

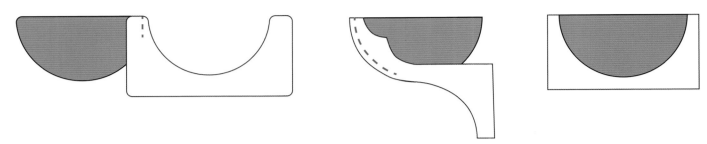

1. With RST, place Template C on top of Template D as shown in the diagram. Then, using a ¼" (6mm) seam, take a few stitches to stabilize the edge of the curve. I prefer to sew curves using the No-Pin Method on page 147, but use your favorite method for sewing curves.

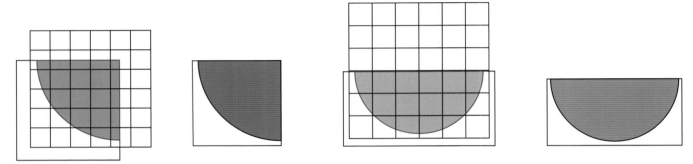

2. Trim the quarter-circle blocks to 3½" x 3½" (8.9 x 8.9cm) and the half-circle blocks to 3½" x 2" (8.9 x 5cm). Be sure to leave ¼" (6mm) seam allowance around the quarter-circles and half-circles.

Quilt Top Assembly

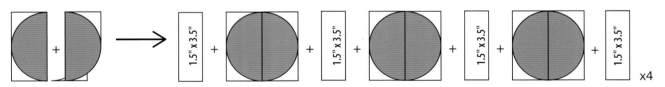

1. Sew together the half-circles to make twelve full circles. Press the seams open. Take four 1½" x 3½" (4 x 8.9cm) background pieces and sew them in between three full circles and on either end of the strip. Make four of these strips.

2. Begin assembling your quilt top! This quilt top will come together in long, thin rows. Sewing these rows together in alternating directions will prevent the rows from warping. I suggest pressing the seams open between the long rows. Use the diagram on page 149 to lay out the pieces.

3. Sew the pieces into rows as shown in the diagram and then join the rows together. The right and left sections are constructed in the same way.

4. Quilt and bind as desired.

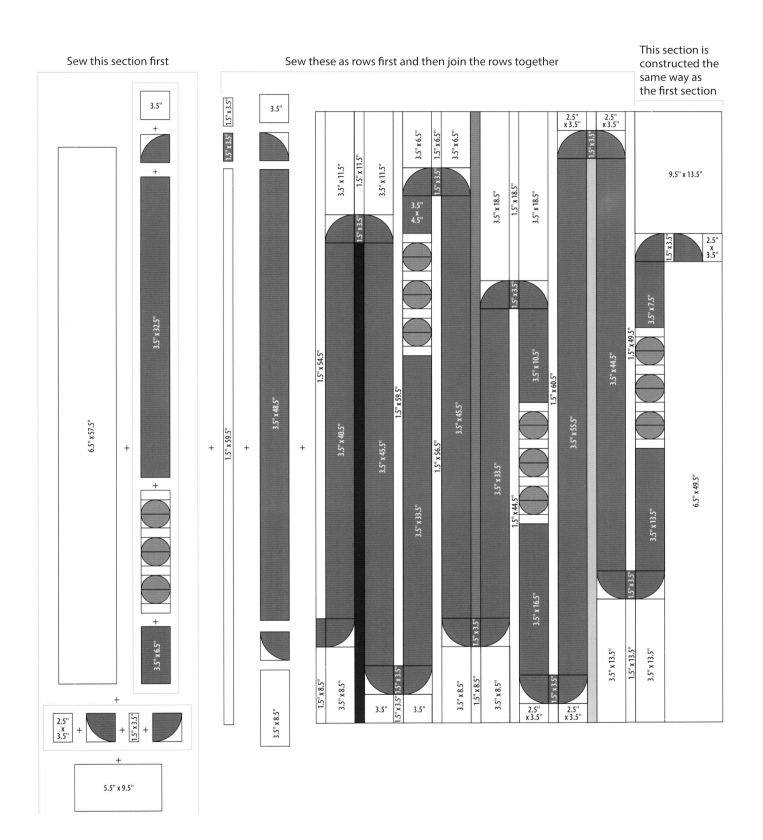

Templates

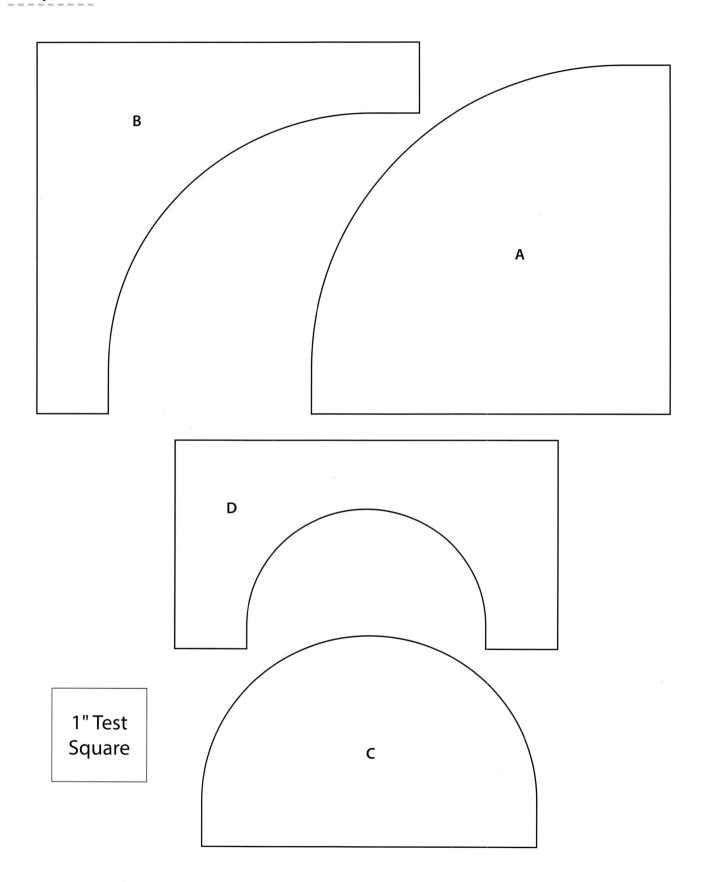

B

A

D

C

1" Test
Square

This finished quilt is an amazing statement piece to liven up your home.

Wax and Wane

By Julie Brown of Luz y Sombra Fiber Art Co.

Wax and Wane is a modern pattern featuring blocks of half-circles arranged to represent the waning and waxing moon. The design offers a reflection on the cyclical and transitional nature of all things. This is a great quilt for the beginner or experienced quilter looking to build confidence in sewing curves.

MATERIALS NEEDED

- See Fabric Requirements below
- Rotary cutter
- Cutting mat
- Fabric scissors
- Fabric marking pen
- Needle
- Thread
- Pins
- Quilting ruler
- Batting

Before You Start

- Read the entire pattern first.
- The finished quilt is 60" x 60" (152.4 x 152.4cm)
- The WOF is assumed to be 42" (106.7cm).
- The seam allowance is ¼" (6mm) unless otherwise noted.
- Sew all pieces RST.
- This pattern includes curved templates.
- Print templates at 100 percent, not "fit to page." Measure the 1" (2.5cm) reference square on your printout to ensure that everything is the correct size.
- Share this quilt on Instagram using the hashtag #WaxAndWaneQuilt.

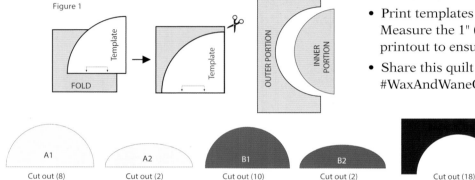

Figure 1

A1 — Cut out (8)
A2 — Cut out (2)
B1 — Cut out (10)
B2 — Cut out (2)
Cut out (18)

FABRIC REQUIREMENTS

Fabric A	¾ yd. (68.6cm)
Fabric B	⅞ yd. (80cm)
Fabric C	3¼ yds. (3m)
Backing	3⅞ yds. (3.5m)
Binding	½ yd. (45.7cm)

CUTTING INSTRUCTIONS

A

Cut three 6½" (16.5cm) x WOF, Subcut:
Eight 6½" x 13" (16.5 x 33cm)

Fold each 6½" x 13" (16.5 x 33cm) rectangle in half and cut out a half-circle using Template A. Discard the outer portions. Label these A1.

Cut One 4" (10cm) x WOF, Subcut:
Two 4" x 13" (10 x 33cm)

Fold each 4" x 13" (10 x 33cm) rectangle in half and cut out the curved piece using Template C. Discard the outer portions. Label these A2.

B

Cut four 6½" (16.5cm) x WOF, Subcut:
Ten 6½" x 13" (16.5 x 33cm)
Two 4" x 13" (10 x 33cm)

Fold each 6½" x 13" (16.5 x 33cm) rectangle in half and cut out a half-circle using Template A. Discard the outer portions. Label these B1.

Fold each 4" x 13" (10 x 33cm) rectangle in half and cut out a curved piece using Template C. Discard the outer portions. Label these B2.

C

Cut nine 9½" (24.1cm) x WOF, Subcut:
Eighteen 9½" x 18½" (24.1 x 47cm)

Fold each 9½" x 18½" (24.1 x 47cm) rectangle in half and cut out a half-circle using Template B. Discard the inner portions. Label these Background.

Cut six 3½" (8.9cm) x WOF

Binding

Cut seven 2½" (6cm) x WOF

Sewing Half-Circles

Sewing curves takes practice and patience to master! The best advice: go slowly and give yourself some grace.

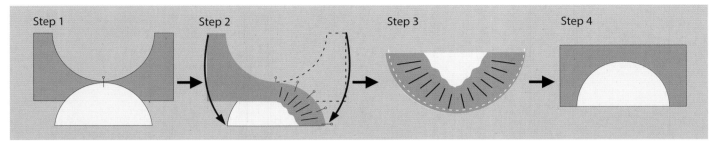

1. Mark the center of your half-circle and background piece by folding it in half. Pin the half-circle and the background piece RST at the center mark.

2. Starting at the center point, match the edges of the curve together until you get to the end, easing the curves together and being mindful not to stretch. Pin as liberally as you like along the curve and at the end point. Repeat on the other side of the curve.

3. Starting at one end, sew slowly along the curve using a ¼" (6mm) seam allowance. Stop as often as needed to adjust and make sure the edges are aligned.

4. Press the seams toward the background fabric.

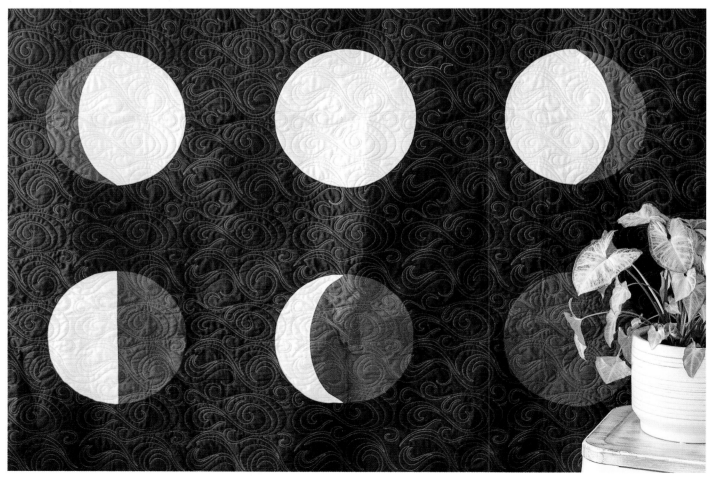

The quilting on this finished piece resembles waves, adding a hint of the moon's relation to the tides.

Piecing Blocks

This quilt is made of four blocks. Each unfinished block measures 9½" x 18½" (24.1 x 47cm).

Block 1

1. Sew eight A1 half-circles to eight Background rectangles. Label six as Block 1.

2. Set aside two blocks to construct Block 3.

Block 2

1. Sew ten B1 half-circles to ten Background rectangles. Label eight as Block 2.

2. Set aside two blocks to construct Block 4.

Block 3

1. Gather the two set-aside blocks constructed for Block 1. Fold each block in half and cut out a curved piece using Template D (see Figure 2 below).

2. Sew the two A2 pieces into the curve.

Block 4

1. Gather the two set-aside blocks constructed for Block 2. Fold each block in half and cut out a curved piece using Template D (see Figure 2 below).

2. Sew the two B2 pieces into the curve.

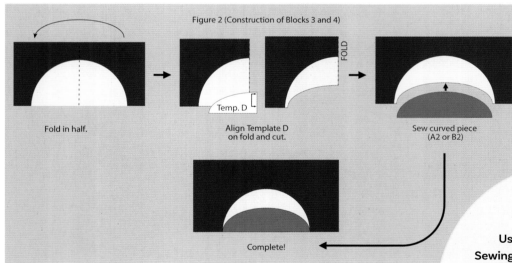

Figure 2 (Construction of Blocks 3 and 4)

Fold in half.

Align Template D on fold and cut.

FOLD

Temp. D

Sew curved piece (A2 or B2)

Complete!

TIP

Use the same steps in the Sewing Half-Circles section to sew the curved pieces. There will be a gap between the points of the "crescent" and the bottom edge of the fabric to account for the seam allowance when sewing the blocks together. Press the seams toward the darker fabric.

Quilt Top Assembly

1. Sew the individual blocks together into rows according to the diagram. Pin at the points where the half-circles meet to ensure that the seams match. Press the seams open.

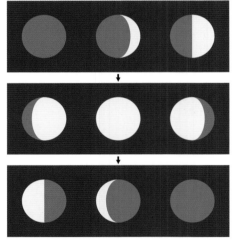

2. Sew the completed rows together, pinning to match at the seams. Press the seams open.

3. Sew the border around the quilt top.

Figure 3

A. Sew all the 3½" (8.9cm) strips together to make one long 3½" (8.9cm) strip. To do this, place RST at a 90-degree angle and sew diagonally as shown in Figure 3. Trim the seam to ¼" (6mm). Press the seams open.

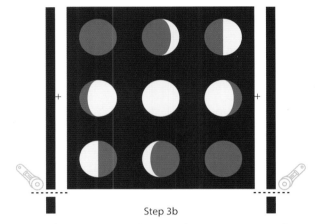

Step 3b

B. Sew the 3½" (8.9cm) strip that you prepared in Step 3A to the left edge of the quilt top, lining up the short edge of the strip with the top edge of the quilt top. Cut the excess to match the bottom edge of the quilt top, as shown in the diagram. Press the seam open. Repeat with the right edge.

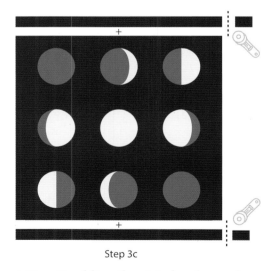

Step 3c

C. Repeat Step B, adding the strip border to the top and bottom edges of the quilt.

Finishing Your Quilt

1. Piece the backing fabric together so that it is large enough to cover the entire back of the quilt. Cut one piece each of batting and backing fabric to be a few inches longer on each side than your quilt top. Be sure your backing fabric and quilt top are well pressed.

2. Smooth out the backing on the floor, wrong side up, and secure the edges with tape. Lay the piece of batting on top and then the quilt top, right side up. Smooth out all layers so they lay flat.

3. Baste using your preferred method and machine- or hand-quilt as desired.

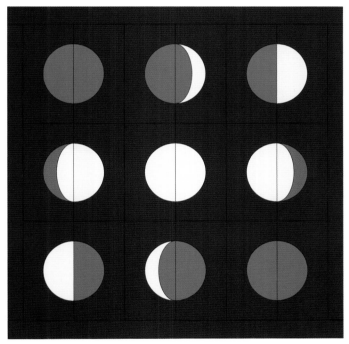

4. Square up the corners and trim the excess batting and backing from the edges of your quilt.

5. To bind your quilt, sew the 2½" (6cm) strips of binding together on the diagonal. Trim to ¼" (6mm) and press. Fold the binding strip in half, wrong sides facing, and line up the long raw edges. Press well.

6. Sew the binding to the quilt, matching the raw edges. Wrap the folded edge of the binding over the raw edge of the quilt top. Machine- or hand-stitch the binding to the back of your quilt.

One of the best ways to display a gorgeous statement quilt in your home is with a decorative ladder set against the wall. See page 171 for more ideas.

Templates

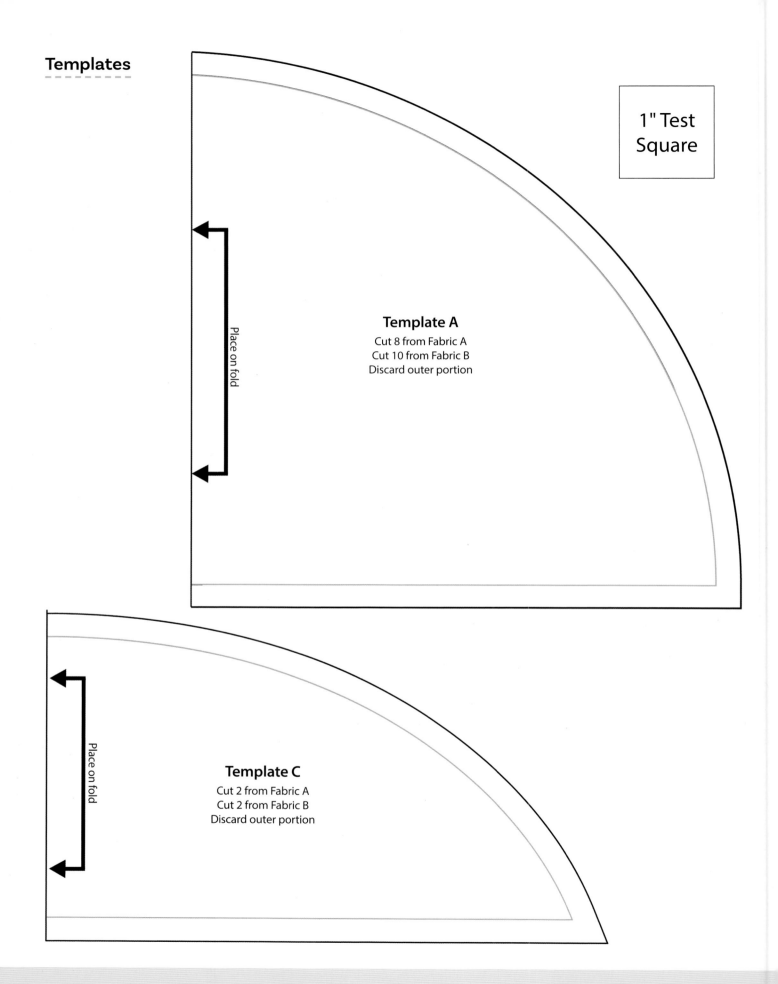

1" Test Square

Template A
Cut 8 from Fabric A
Cut 10 from Fabric B
Discard outer portion

Place on fold

Template C
Cut 2 from Fabric A
Cut 2 from Fabric B
Discard outer portion

Place on fold

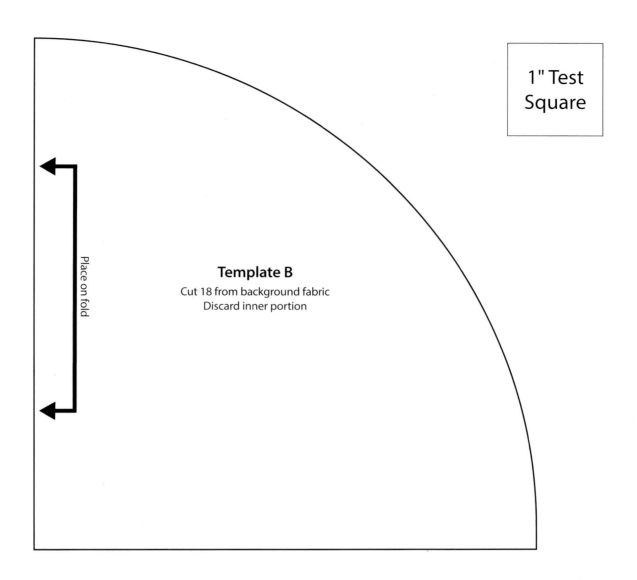

Template B

Cut 18 from background fabric
Discard inner portion

Place on fold

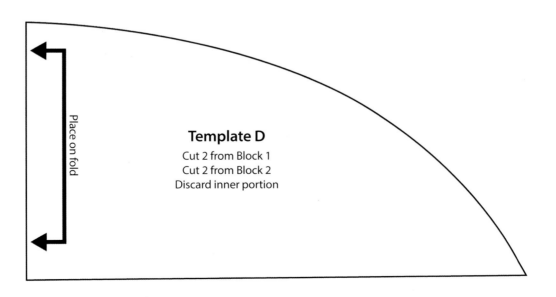

Template D

Cut 2 from Block 1
Cut 2 from Block 2
Discard inner portion

Place on fold

V. After the Quilting

The process of completing your art and caring for your art is just as important as the process of creating it! Spending hours of time creating something beautiful only to throw it on a top shelf of your garage is—I think we can all agree—a grievous crime! This section will cover some of our best tips, tricks, and ideas for finishing your art and helping it stand the test of time.

The ways you bind, display, wash, and store your quilts will greatly affect their longevity.

Put It on My Tab Tutorial: How to Add Tabs to Your Mini Quilt

By Casey Cometti of Wellspring Design

You've almost finished your mini quilt (don't attach the binding yet!) and can already envision how lovely it will look in the living room, the nursery, a friend's house, etc., when it occurs to you: "How am I going to hang this on the wall?" If, like me, you break into a cold sweat when your partner suggests hammering a nail through a completed quilt, this tutorial is for you. Some methods to secure a quilt, like a hanging sleeve or fabric pockets on the corners, are better for large quilts and often involve fitting a hanging rod through the quilt. The following method uses bias tape to create tabs that are secured into the binding to facilitate hanging without special gadgets.

WHAT YOU'LL NEED

- One 1" x 12" (2.5 x 30.5cm) strip of fabric
  (if you would like extra tabs for future use, cut a longer strip)

- Rotary cutter

- Ruler

- ½" (1.5cm) bias tape maker

- Iron

- Basic sewing machine

- Pins

- Wool pressing mat (optional)

1. Take a 1" (2.5cm) strip of fabric and feed it through the large end of the bias tape maker. If using a patterned fabric, be sure to insert the fabric wrong side up into the bias tape maker. As it comes out, notice that the fabric has folded over on itself.

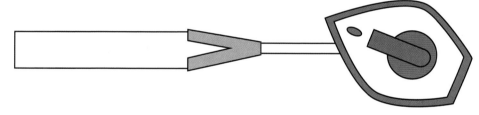

2. With the iron and optional wool pressing mat, gently press the fabric as it exits the bias tape maker.

3. Fold the pressed bias tape in half, so the folded edges align and the raw edges are tucked inside.

4. Stitch the two folded edges together.

5. Cut two 3" (7.6cm) strips from the sewn bias tape. Reserve the rest for another project.

6. Measure 4" (10cm) from each edge of the mini quilt and pin the 3" (7.6cm) bias tape pieces to the back of the wall hanging, as pictured. Be sure the bias tape lies flat and is not twisted. Once it is pinned, measure the distance from the edge of the mini quilt to the center of the bias tape again to make sure it is uniform. (You can center one tab in the middle of the wall hanging; however, I've found it easier to hang a mini quilt level with two tabs.)

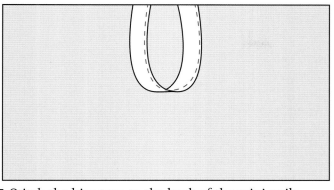 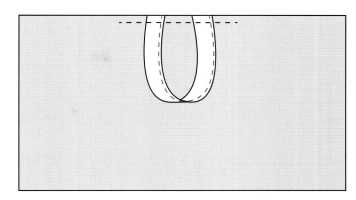

7. Stitch the bias tape to the back of the mini quilt.

8. Attach the binding to the front of the quilt as usual, taking care to stitch over the attached tabs.

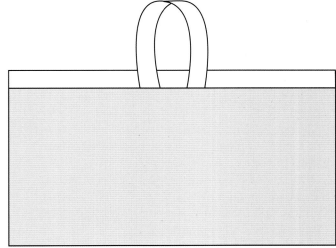

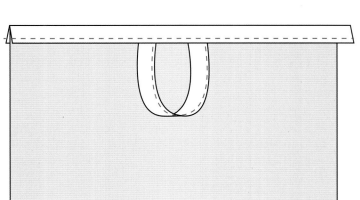

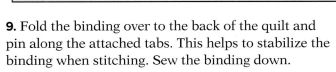

9. Fold the binding over to the back of the quilt and pin along the attached tabs. This helps to stabilize the binding when stitching. Sew the binding down.

10. You're ready to hang your quilt. The tabs will lay flat on the back of the mini quilt until it is time to secure the quilt to the wall.

TIP

I generally hand-bind my projects, but I recommend machine-binding when attaching these tabs. It secures the tabs and prevents tension on the binding while the mini quilt is hanging.

Bias Binding Tutorial

By Karen Wade of Bessie Pearl

You've mastered curves, hexagons, and the perennial fan-favorite (or nemesis)—the HST. Quilting is always about shapes: cutting up one shape and sewing it to another to end up with a whole new shape. And often, at the end, you're left with a quilt with four straight sides, ready for binding. But sometimes not. A circular tree skirt, an EPP hexagon quilt, rounded corners—all of these call for a different type of binding for finishing. Enter bias binding.

What Is Bias Binding and Why Does it Matter?

Bias binding looks just like regular quilt binding, but instead of being cut on the straight grain, it is cut on the bias, or at a 45-degree angle to the selvage. Cutting the fabric on this angle allows the fibers to stretch, giving your binding the ease and ability to go around curved edges smoothly and still lay flat. Other bias binding benefits include:

- Fabric cut on the bias wears longer. Often, the edges of a quilt are the first to show wear and tear, so finishing any quilt with bias binding helps to preserve all the hard work you've put into it!

- It doesn't fray! I don't know about you, but anything that means fewer strings I have to trim is good in my book.

- Cutting a printed fabric on the bias will change the direction of the print and adds an interesting detail to your quilt. For example, I love to use plaids as backings on my quilt. Then, for the binding, I'll use the same fabric but cut it on the bias. The binding will match my backing, but it has a less "matchy" finish.

Bias binding does have a few downsides, however:

- It can take more time to make. Yes, there are definitely more steps to making bias binding and a bit more fabric geometry to think about, but once you do it a few times, it gets easier—I promise!

- It wastes some fabric. There will be some fabric that gets cut off and is left unused. You may also end up with more binding than you need. Most of us don't need yards and yards of binding for our project, and a yard of fabric can make up to 20 yards of bias binding! Choosing a neutral fabric for your binding and using it on several projects can help offset the waste that comes from the excess binding.

When cutting your fabric into strips for bias binding, you can choose a trade-off. Option 1: You can use a smaller piece of fabric to save on waste, but you'll have shorter strips and more seams. Option 2: You can use a larger piece of fabric, resulting in longer strips and fewer seams, but more waste. The method I explain here in my tutorial reduces the amount of waste for any size fabric you choose.

Cutting a printed fabric on the bias changes the direction of the print— an easy trick for creating interesting details on a finished quilt.

What's Next?

Use one of the two methods that follow. The first tutorial is the strip method, followed by a tutorial on continuous bias binding.

Bias Binding with Strips

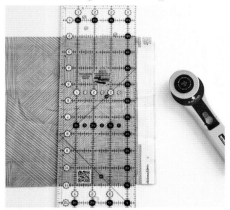

1. Trim off the selvage.

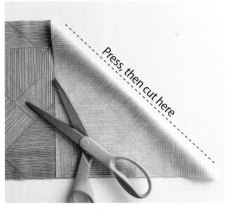

2. Lay out your fabric, right side up. Fold the right top corner down to meet the bottom edge. Press that edge (either finger-press or use your iron), then open your fabric back up and cut along the fold line.

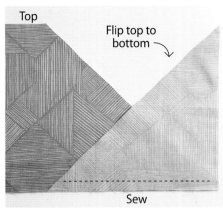

3. Holding the top edges of your cut triangle, flip it over and line it up with the bottom edges of your other piece. Sew the two pieces together and press your seam open.

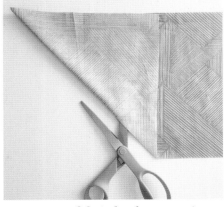

4. Lay your fabric back out again, right side up. This time take the *bottom left* corner and fold it up to the top edge. Press with your finger or iron and then cut along the fold line. Flip the straight edge of the cut triangle up to the top and sew. Press the seam open.

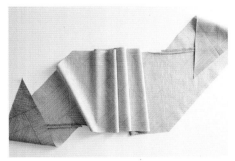

5. When you're done, you will have a really weird-looking shape. It's OK!

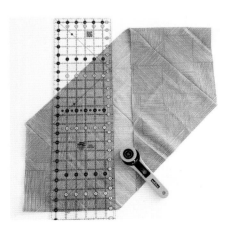

6. Lay it out right side down and fold the ends in toward the center.

7. Turn your work 45 degrees so that the raw diagonal edges are now straight up and down. Line up your ruler with one of the raw edges and start cutting 2½" (6cm) strips (or your preferred binding width).

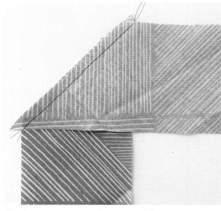

8. You will end up with a variety of different lengths of strips that you will sew together end to end in the following steps.

9. Line up the diagonal edges of two strips, RST, ¼" (6mm) away from the corner. The strips will lay perpendicular to each other, and you will have small corner overhangs as shown.

10. Sew your strips together using a ¼" (6mm) seam allowance. The important thing is to start and end your seam where the strips cross to ensure that your binding strips line up evenly.

11. Continue this process until all the strips are sewn into one continuous piece (feel free to chain-stitch them!). Trim off the dog-ears in line with the strip. Finish by folding and ironing in half lengthwise.

Bias binding is best to use when your pieces have a curved or scalloped edge, as it molds more easily around those shapes.

Continuous Bias Binding Tutorial

By Kiley Ferons of Kiley's Quilt Room

The benefit of this method is not having to piece together your strips one at a time. Magical, right? However, you have to hand-cut the strips with scissors—which is a bummer, I know. We cut 16" (40.6cm) x WOF for this example. It will be cut into a 16" x 16" (40.6 x 40.6cm) square, which yields 2½ yds. (2.3m) of binding. The larger the square, the more binding it will yield.

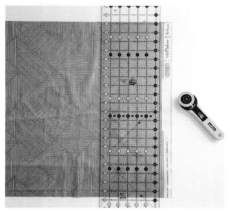

1. Cut off the selvage using a quilting ruler and rotary cutter.

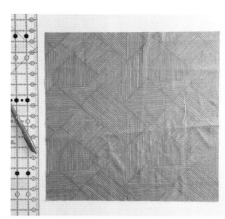

2. Cut your piece of fabric into a square. This is a 16" x 16" (40.6 x 40.6cm) square.

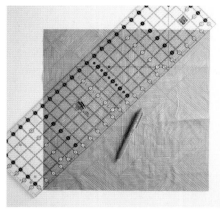

3. Using your ruler, draw a line from one corner to the opposite diagonal corner.

4. Mark the top and bottom of your square with an *X* anywhere along the edge.

5. Cut along the diagonal line with a rotary blade or scissors.

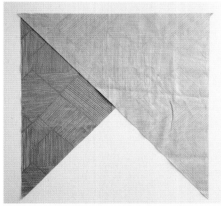

6. Align both edges marked with an *X*, RST. Be sure to offset the top piece by ¼" (6mm). Sew along this top edge.

7. Press the seams open. You should now have a nice parallelogram shape.

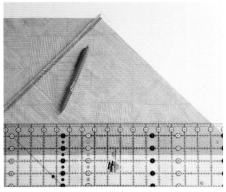

8. With your ruler, measure from the bottom edge up by however wide you want to cut your binding. I like to cut at 2½" (6cm). Draw a line every 2½" (6cm) or however wide you want your binding. Continue until you reach the top of your fabric (you may have some extra fabric at the top—that's OK!).

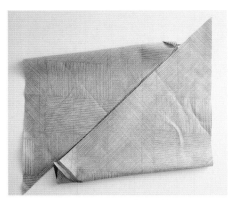

9. With the fabric right side up, pull the points in along their edges so that you now have a diagonal opening in your fabric. All your drawn lines should match up. Then pull both corners diagonally so that the lines now match up with the next line over, creating one continuous line on your fabric.

10. Pin this edge together by poking a pin through the fabric ¼" (6mm) down from the edge along one of the lines. Then poke it through the other edge ¼" (6mm) down on the line it matches up with. Do the same with each line. Sew along this edge. If you used a heat-erasable pen, do not press your seam until the end.

11. Begin cutting along the continuous line, making sure that you don't cut through both layers of fabric at the same time. Continue cutting around until you get to the end.

12. You will have an end that is too skinny. Just pick that seam out and toss the scraps.

13. Press the seams open and press the binding in half lengthwise. Now you are ready to bind any shape!

Quilt Care and Display

Many people make the follow common mistakes, but this section will help you avoid them:

- Not using your quilts! They are made with love and are meant to be loved.

- Colors bleeding—don't let it happen to you!

- Never washing your quilts. Ewww!

Note: All of the following tips and steps are for new quilts, *not* antique quilts! Antique quilts require a much gentler process that is not covered here.

Washing Your Quilts

Many people seem to be nervous about washing their quilts. We are here to dispel some myths and give you the steps you need to confidently wash those quilts. Properly caring for your quilts will extend their life and keep them "healthy."

Did you know that during the cotton-making process, tension is applied to the fibers of the cotton? This makes it nice and flat and ready to use. However, when you wash your cotton, the heat from the washer and/or dryer releases the tension in the fibers and causes it to shrink some. This is a normal process and is to be expected.

Because of this, many people prefer to prewash their fabrics before cutting them or otherwise using them. But I want to normalize the fact that "ain't nobody got time for that!" You will never catch me prewashing my fabric. Plus, if you do prewash your fabric, you won't get that same crinkly, yummy goodness after you wash the whole quilt—which is a must!

A lot of people preach handwashing only for quilts. But it is definitely OK to put your quilts in the washing

You can wash your quilts in the washing machine—just be careful to use the gentle cycle and cold water.

machine. That's what I do (because, again, ain't nobody got time for that!) Just be sure to use a gentle cycle. If you want to handwash your quilt and you have the time for it, be careful not to wring or twist the quilt when getting the water out. Just use a gentle squeeze. You don't want to permanently damage the fibers of the fabric.

The first thing to remember when washing a quilt is to use *cold* water. Using cold water will help reduce shrinking and will also help decrease the chances of any colors bleeding. If you are concerned about color bleeding (for example, when you have a lot of contrasting colors, like whites and darks), throw in a couple of "color catcher" sheets (or the whole box if you are really worried!) These sheets will absorb any dye that gets leaked into the water.

When you are done washing your quilt, it is time to dry it. You can certainly use the dryer on a low heat or "air-dry" setting. If that makes you too nervous, or you like to use fresh air for drying, lay the quilt flat on some grass to dry. To air-dry indoors, lay the quilt on a bed or

> ## TIP
>
> If you are making a quilt as more of an art piece, you may want to either prewash your fabrics or just spot-clean the piece to keep all the fabrics nice, crisp, and flat.

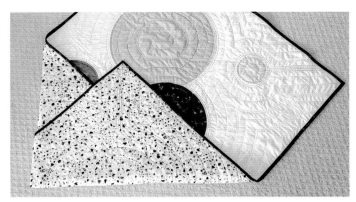

2. Fold the other bottom corner up to the middle.

clean floor. If you do take your quilt outside to dry, be sure it's not a sunny day. Sun can cause color fading. I would also recommend that you not use a clothesline or clips to hang the quilt to dry as it will warp the quilt and could cause permanent damage.

Once your quilt is clean and dry, you can put it right back to regular use! However, if you are like me, and you rotate your quilts and store the ones that are not in use, you can fold it up and put it away.

Folding Your Quilts

Believe it or not, there is a right way and a wrong way to fold a quilt. If you fold a quilt the same way you fold any other blanket or throw, don't worry—so do most people! But there is a better way. Typically, quilts are made on a straight grain. Folding the grains in half, and then in half again, and then in half again, on repeat, can damage the fibers over time. Instead, fold the quilt on the bias to keep the fibers healthy and intact. Here's how:

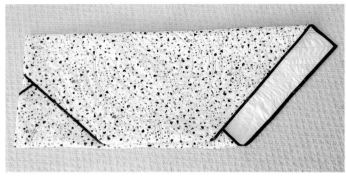

3. Bring a top corner down toward the center to meet the opposite fold.

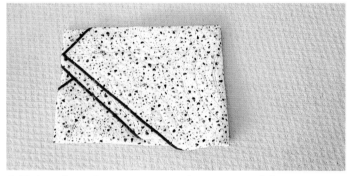

4. Bring the other top corner down toward the center to meet the opposite fold.

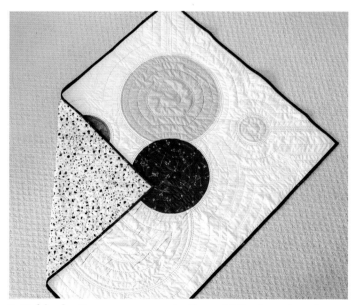

1. Fold a bottom corner up to the middle, keeping the angles at 45 degrees.

TIP

Unfold your quilts to let them air out and then refold them differently on occasion to prevent permanent creases form forming.

5. Fold in half and in half again until it fits in your storage area.

Storing Your Quilts

Storing your quilts properly is also key to their longevity. Do not store them in a spot that gets direct sunlight, as this will cause the colors to fade and the fabrics to weaken. Choose a cabinet, closet, chest, or drawer that faces indirect light or no light, is easy to access (so you can use and show off those beautiful quilts), is in a controlled climate, and is not susceptible to moisture.

How to Display Your Quilts

"Cozy" is a word I like to use when describing how I want my home to feel. I want to feel relaxed in my home, and I want my guests to feel welcome and immediately comfortable when they're over. Quilts play into this vibe so well! There is nothing cozier than a soft homemade quilt. I've been quilting for several years now, and, because of that, I have a small army of quilts just begging to be displayed around my house—you know, for snuggling with and making everything super cozy. When cold weather approaches, it's an especially good time to break out your favorite quilts and display them (and all your hard work) around your house. Here are some of my favorite ways to display quilts:

A SPECIAL NOTE ON CATALOGING QUILTS

Cataloging quilts is a great idea and strongly encouraged! It's a good way to keep track of how many quilts you have made, who you made them for, what patterns and fabrics you used, and other notes, like what you felt or thought about during the process.

It's OK if you haven't been cataloging your quilts all along. And don't feel overwhelmed by starting now. The My Quilts app is a fantastic resource for journaling, cataloging, and tracking quilt projects. It's free to use, and you can enter as many projects as you want. You can even get inspiration for more projects on the public wall. Download the app by searching for "My Quilts" in your app store.

Blanket Ladders

I *love* throwing a quilt on a blanket ladder and placing it in a room. Your eye is immediately drawn to it upon entering the space and is a great way to highlight a favorite quilt. If you have a larger blanket ladder, you can use it to display multiple quilts.

A beautiful quilt artistically spilling out of a basket ready for use adds a lovely, inviting touch to any room.

Try building your own gallery wall out of complementary mini designs.

Decorative cabinets with glass or mesh doors keep your quilts ready for use and create vibrant focal points.

Decorative quilts and beds are a combination that will never go out of style.

Couches

This one may seem obvious, but it's a must! Drape quilts over your couches, and you can switch out which quilts are displayed throughout the year to coordinate with the seasons or holidays.

Beds

Beds and quilts are a match made in heaven! Toss one on your bed after you make it in the morning and see how happy you feel every time you enter your bedroom.

Cabinets

Do you have *a lot* of quilts in your home? A cabinet with glass doors allows you (and your guests) to see the quilts inside, so it serves as storage and decor at the same time.

Walls

There are some very cute, modern wooden quilt hangers out there that you can use to display an entire quilt on your wall. This is a fun and dramatic way to display your quilt. It's like having a custom piece of artwork on your wall, and the best part is that you made it!

If you like to make mini quilts or wall hangings, and you can't choose which ones to display, a gallery wall is a great option. You can mix and match your quilts with other types of wall decor such as signs, framed pictures, hanging plants, etc., to create depth and contrast in your gallery.

Index

About the Authors and Contributors

Kiley Ferons

Editor-in-Chief and founder of *Modish Quilter Magazine*, Kiley Ferons has been quilting since 2011, when she was pregnant with her first child and decided to make her a quilt. She quickly fell in love with the art form and evolved her hobby into a longarming business in 2015. In 2020, she began designing and writing her own quilt patterns and, in 2023, published her first book, *Modern Day Quilter*. She also designs fabric for Moda. You can find more of her work at: *https://kileysquiltroom.com/* and on Instagram: @kileysquiltroom

Megan Saenz

Co-editor and photographer of *Modish Quilter Magazine*, Megan Saenz bought her first sewing machine when she was pregnant with her first baby so she could make baby clothes. In 2019, she was introduced to quilting and quickly fell in love. She loves using bright, fun colors with modern designs. A self-taught photographer, she has found her niche as a quilt photographer and loves taking pictures in beautiful outdoor places. You can find more of her work on Instagram: @megsaenz and @the_quiltographer

Elyse Thompson

Modish Quilter Magazine's art director, graphic artist, and illustrator Elyse Thompson fell into the world of graphic design by luck. While not a quilter herself, she grew up in the quilting world and merged her love of art with quilting through the magazine. Her favorite part of quilting is choosing the color scheme and patterns that help shape the look and feel of the quilt. You can find more of her work at *https://www.elystrations.com* and on Instagram: @ElyseThompDesign

Contributing Designers

Julie Brown—*Wax and Wane pattern on page 152*

Julie creates representational landscape quilts that are designed to help people feel more connected to nature. She has also discovered ways to naturally dye her own fabrics, which you can see showcased in all her quilts. You can find more of her work at *https://juliraeart.com/*

Casey Cometti—*hanging tabs tutorial on page 162*

Casey Cometti of Wellspring Design began quilting in 2016 as a creative outlet in her busy life as a mom of four. Casey has a distinctive Southwestern style that her followers have come to know and love. In 2023, she also became a fabric designer for Riley Blake. You can find her work at *https://wellspringdesignsquilting.com/*

Erin Grogan—*Infinity Mini pattern on page 54, Tidal Bloom pattern on page 82, and couching tutorial on page 92*

Erin started quilting in 2017, and she left her corporate job in January of 2020 to focus on growing her business and dream: Love Sew Modern. Erin worked very closely with *Modish Quilter Magazine* for a long time and made many contributions to the publication. You can find more of her work at *https://www.lovesewmodern.com/*

Cindy Hilfiger—*Rainbow Cotton Pottery pattern on page 32*

Cindy Hilfiger is both a creator and a longarm quilter. She does beautiful scrappy work in her quilting and adds a unique flare to each quilt with her longarming. True to her scrappy signature style, she created "cotton pottery," where she wraps cording in scraps to make bowls. You can find more of her work at *https://longarmquilter.net/*

Elza McKenna—*Wandering pattern on page 144*

Elza started quilting in 2012 and has spent her time fine-tuning her unique geometric and modern style of quilting. She has an eye for creating movement in the geometric shapes with which she designs her quilts that is captivating and inspiring. You can find more of her work at *https://www.rippeystreetquilts.com/*

Meghan Morris—*Orchid Garden pattern on page 118*

Meghan started her quilting journey at the age of ten but has truly come into her own as a quilter since 2010. She has a beautiful way of tying the traditional to the modern. You can find more of her work at *https://www.apieceofquietquilts.com/*

Pascaline—*Drum Pillow pattern on page 12*

Pascaline is a graphic artist who creates stunning whimsical art that she incorporates into her fiber creations. She creates garment patterns for children, Cricut designs, and illustrations. She has done several collaborations with quilters as well. You can see more of her work at *https://www.pompomdumonde.com/*

Jess Poémape—*Metztli pattern on page 62*

Jess has been quilting since she was fifteen. At the age of sixteen, she won an international youth competition, and her quilt was hung in a museum in Salt Lake City, Utah. After a decade of quilting, she finally started designing her own patterns and has been creating beautiful quilting art ever since. You can find more of her work at *https://www.etsy.com/shop/jesspoemape/* and on Instagram: jesspoemape

Karen Wade—*bias binding tutorial on page 164*

Karen found her own unique business niche as a curator of premade bindings for quilters. She takes pride in her brand, and it shows in her products! She offers a wide variety of bindings that are beautiful and timeless. You can find more of her work at *https://bessie pearlbindingco.com/*